CONCEPTUAL APPROACHES TO

Elementary Particle Physics

Stephen Melton

For my mother, Pam…

whose handwritten study notes I found buried in the first scientific book I ever wrote, confirming my theory that she is the purest and most beautiful system of subatomic particles nature ever produced.

CONTENTS

Introduction

ll physics aims to describe and explain the natural world, simply because humans are inherently curious beings with an undying need to know how things work. Where astrophysics and cosmology work to describe the universe on the grandest of scales, particle physics explores the smallest most fundamental pieces of the world; the subatomic pieces so small they cannot be reduced to anything simpler. Particle physics is often referred to as high energy physics because the conditions under which we study matter at fundamental levels resemble those of the extremely hot and dense newborn universe just fractions of a second after the Big Bang. As we will also find for ourselves, producing even elementary amounts of mass in nature requires relatively tremendous quantities of energy.

Humans are also naturally skeptical and are wired to question anything beyond the bounds of our everyday experiences, which is why we developed the scientific method. Even the most sensible hypothesis about how the world works, in and of itself, is not enough and must be test against nature herself to know for sure. Only those hypotheses backed by sufficient experimental evidence can be elevated to a genuine law or principle for describing the natural world. Even still, our constantly increasing abilities to probe nature to ever deeper levels means that our laws and principles themselves are subject to ongoing scrutiny. In this way, all physics, including particle physics, is a matter of theory and experiment. Where the innovative and sometimes downright bizarre ideas of theorists drive our understanding of the world forward, the rigor of experimentalists are constantly grooming them to ensure only the most tried-and-true set of laws.

Above all else, any truly valid scientific theory, no matter how revolutionary, must be in complete agreement with the ideas and principles we already know to be true and well tested against experiment evidence. The two primary frameworks or pillars of modern physics are Albert Einstein's relativity theory and quantum mechanics.

Special relativity unites the formerly separate ideas of space and time into a single dynamic spacetime fabric that stretches or contorts to ensure all observers measure an identical velocity of light. From this arise several shocking revelations, including the equivalence of mass and energy, expressed through the most famous equation in the world, E = mc2. The strange effects of relativity manifest themselves only at ultra-high velocities, making them critical in describing subatomic particles moving at significant — or in some cases true — light speed.

Quantum mechanics describes the motions and behaviors of matter and energy at fundamental scales. As we will learn from chapter two, the laws governing the motions of atoms and particles are entirely different from those governing the motion of ordinary objects. Nevertheless, even the strange principles of quantum mechanics must agree with the principles of special relativity, and vice versa.

This leads to the honest question of why anyone should care about invisible atoms and particles in the first place? What have we gained from obsessively studying nature for millennia? The question should rightfully be, "how could anyone not care about particles?" Fundamentally speaking, every person, planet, star and galaxy in the universe are just huge messes of the same handful of atoms and particles, held together by a few forces. As a human being, to not take even a slight interest in these fundamental building blocks of nature is to be an author without understanding the letters of the alphabet, or a chef that never learned about the basic ingredients.

On a more practical level, the principles of particle physics serve as the scientific underpinnings of the entire modern world, from your smartphone and all electronics to artificial intelligence and life-saving medical equipment. None of the advancements in these and many other fields would have been possible without our knowledge of the atom and its subatomic components.

It is also true that particle physics is no simple matter and requires decades of difficult mathematics and training to practice at a professional level. The purpose of this book is to provide general conceptual knowledge of what the complicated equations and data tell us at an introductory level. By taking a conceptual (and often visual) approach, we are spared the brutal technicalities but can still achieve a thorough and comprehensive understanding of particle physics.

Our journey begins with the building blocks of matter, from the general atomic structure all the way down to the truly elementary particles that are unable to be reduced to anything simpler. We will become briefly acquainted with the interesting palette of particle types, learning about their basic physical properties and general classifications.

Next, we unpack the basic and most important principles of quantum mechanics, the rules governing the subatomic world. Almost entirely different from the laws governing our everyday world, quantum mechanics reveals the inherently uncertain and probabilistic nature of the universe. Not only will these laws help us develop a modernized atomic model, but they also form the underpinnings of all other discussions along the way.

Chapter three introduces us to the fundamental forces, or "interactions," between the elementary particles, from the directly familiar electromagnetic force, through the two invisible but equally important so-called "strong" and "weak" nuclear forces. Applying a modern quantum mechanical approach will help us describe each interaction in detail and allow us to classify the elementary particles. We will also rely heavily on the idea of fields, which will prove to be the most fundamental aspect of all interactions.

We then briefly detour to explore the many methods by which we detect, study and even create subatomic particles. This includes surveying some of the most common particle detectors and accelerators, how they work and some of the landmark discoveries to which they have led. This will also take us beyond the building blocks of ordinary matter to explore high-energy and short-lived exotic particles.

Our cumulative knowledge will allow us to approach the standard model of particle physics, our grand scientific framework for describing the elementary particles and forces and the laws by which they are governed. Exploring the predictive prowess of the standard model will bring together many important concepts and introduce us to some of universe's deepest and most abstract laws and how they factor into our understanding of nature. We also acknowledge some of the most critical and glaring shortcomings of the standard model in its current state, including the unknown nature of both dark matter and dark energy, as well as its complete omission of all gravitational interactions. Solving these and other mysteries currently "beyond" the standard model serves as the frontier of modern physics.

Matter

The elementary building blocks of nature

The atom

The entirety of the vast physical universe, every planet, star, galaxy, and person, are all comprised of extremely tiny but nevertheless physical objects that we call atoms. They are the building blocks of the more than one hundred chemical elements arranged along the periodic table, both naturally occurring, and synthetic.

The first two elements, hydrogen and helium, are the simplest and most abundant atoms and together account for 98% of normal matter in the universe. The remaining matter is around 1% oxygen and a slew of other trace elements, like carbon and neon. Hydrogen and helium were produced almost 14 billion years ago, fractions of a second after the big bang and creation of the universe. More complex elements, including the ones comprising earth and your own body, were forged by nuclear processes only capable of occurring deep in the cores of stars and spread throughout the universe through violent supernova explosions.

Atoms vary in size but are all roughly one tenth of a billionth of a meter, making them far too small to ever be seen directly with our eyes or even by our most powerful microscopes. Even in an already microscopic object, like a single grain of sand on a beach, there are some 50 quintillion atoms (50 followed by 16 zeros). There are more atoms in your one human body than there are stars in the observable universe. Astronomically large or small factors like these are simply too staggering for our minds to realistically process, yet they are an unavoidable part of investigating the atomic and subatomic world. It will therefore often be essential to make use of scientific notation to help make various numbers more manageable.

Scientific notation

All scientific notations include a ***coefficient*** and an ***exponent***:

The coefficient is the non-zero significant digit or digits in the number, such as the 2 and 4 in 24,000,000, for example. The first number of the coefficient must always be between 1 and 10, so we can move the decimal point to make this 2.4.

The exponent can now be determined by simply counting the number of places the decimal point has moved. In the case of our example the decimal was required to move 7 places to the left. Therefore, 24,000,000 in its scientific notation form is 2.4×10^7.

Scientific notation is also useful for better comprehending extremely small numbers simply by moving the decimal point in the opposite direction and reversing the sign of the exponent. Reversing the sign of the exponent in the previous scientific notation to -7 for example, or 2.4×10^{-7} can now represent the very small number 0.00000024.

We will make frequent use of scientific notation throughout our discussion when referencing the many very large and small atomic and subatomic values.

The word atom comes from the ancient Greek word *atomos* meaning indivisible. However, today we know atoms are not solid and impenetrable, but are themselves intricate systems of even smaller *sub*-atomic particles, namely protons, neutrons, and electrons. In all cases, every atom consists of two regions, a dense central nucleus encircled by outer clouds of electrons.

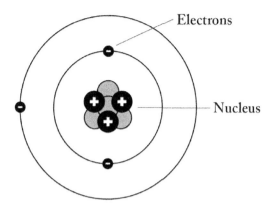

1.1 Simple structural model of the atom representing a central nucleus containing positively charged protons and neutral neutrons, surrounded by outer "orbitals" of negatively charged electrons.

Protons and neutrons are confined to the extremely dense nucleus, which is around 100,000 times smaller than the atom with a diameter of around 10^{-15} meters. Even if you could enlarge an atom to be the size of a professional sporting arena, the nucleus would still only appear as a barely visible pea sitting in the middle of the stadium.

The number of protons in the nucleus determines the type of element, or the atomic number, which in turn determines any element's place among the periodic table. For instance, element number eight, oxygen, is composed of atoms with eight protons in their nuclei.

All protons carry one positive elementary unit of electric charge, labeled *+1 e*, which is considered the tiniest quantity of electricity that can exist freely in nature. They also possess a relatively large mass of just over 938 MeV, making them nearly 2,000 times more massive than electrons and ensuring that well over 99% of the atom's total mass exists crammed within the tiny central nucleus.

Beyond hydrogen, every atomic nucleus also contains at least one neutron, which as its name insinuates carries no charge and is electrically neutral. While neutrons do not affect the net electric charge of an atom, they contain a slightly greater mass than even the proton at over 940 MeV and therefore contribute significantly to the total atomic mass and stability of the nucleus. While the number of protons determines the type of atom and remains the same, most chemical elements also exist in versions with different numbers of neutrons, called *isotopes*. The additional mass from these extra neutrons makes the nuclei of many isotopes highly unstable, causing them to spontaneously transform into lighter and more stable elements through radioactive decay. Some elements, like uranium, have only unstable isotopes and are always radioactive, making them ideal for many things from nuclear reactors to atomic weapons.

All unstable particles in nature have a specific *half-life*, which is the time it takes for roughly half of a sample of the particles to spontaneously decay into lighter more stable particle. The neutron itself has a relatively long half-life of just over 10 minutes, meaning that if you could hypothetically place 100 free neutrons on a table in your laboratory, after roughly 10 minutes 50 of them would have spontaneously decayed into lighter particles, namely a proton and other smaller particles. Alternatively, modern theory and observations both indicate the proton is stable and does not undergo spontaneous decay. If the proton does indeed decay it would have to occur at an extremely slow rate over trillions of years, which is believed to be unlikely. We will take up the particle decay process in greater detail in chapter two when we explore the fundamental forces.

Clouds of tiny electrons orbit rapidly around the nucleus in perfectly equal numbers to protons. Electrons all carry a perfectly equal magnitude but opposite sign of electric charge to the proton, or -1 *e*. With a tiny mass of just 0.511 MeV electrons are believed to be a truly fundamental particle, meaning they have no simpler internal structure to which they can be reduced, they are indivisible.

Electrons circle the nucleus in concentric orbital "shells," each of which can hold a specific number of electrons, the innermost orbital can hold two, the next orbital can hold up to eight, and so on. Unlike protons bound to the nucleus, many occurrences in nature can cause electrons to be added or removed from an atom, known as an *ion*. By gaining or losing an electron, ionized atoms also have either a positive or negative net charge and are electrically unstable.

Electrons in the outermost or **valence** shell can be removed from their orbitals and transferred between atoms, causing the flow of electricity. Materials like copper have atomic structures with free valence electrons which facilitate the flow of electricity and are known as conductors, materials like sulfur that resist the flow are called insulators. Semiconducting materials such as silicon neither completely allow or resist the flow of electricity and can be used to reliably control the currents that power our modern electronics.

Generations of matter

Through the second half of the twentieth century, two additional particles were discovered that are identical in every conceivable way to the electron but possess substantially greater masses. The first, called the **muon** (μ), was detected in the natural cosmic radiation constantly falling on our planet constantly from the depths of space. Muons all have a mass of approximately 106 MeV, making them more than 200 times heavier than the electron. While this mass still pales by comparison to a proton or neutron, it causes them to be highly unstable, decaying into an ordinary electron in two-millionths of a second.

Finally, a third and even more massive version of the electron, called the *tau* (τ), was discovered in the 1970s. With a mass of 1,776 MeV the tau weighs nearly 3,500 times the electron and has a proportionally short lifetime of just 10^{-13} seconds before decaying. However, unlike the muon the relatively large mass of the tau allows it to decay into many possible types of particles, including entire protons and neutrons.

Together, the three versions or *generations* of the electron form a class of matter particles known as *leptons* (from the Greek *leptos* meaning "light" or "thin"). Like the electron itself, both the muon and tau are also fundamental and indivisible particles. However, the increasing mass of each new generation of lepton causes it to be increasingly unstable and therefore have a shorter overall lifetime before decaying into a lighter more stable generation and an associated neutrino, which we will encounter in the following sections.

Especially given their extremely short lifetimes, the overall purpose of these additional heavier generation is currently unknown. Modern theory also indicates no need or existence for any additional generations beyond the electron, muon and tau.

Leptons

Particle	Symbol	Mass	Charge
Electron	e	0.511 MeV	-1
Muon	μ	106 MeV	-1
Tau	τ	1,776 MeV	-1

TABLE 1.1 All three generations of leptons increasing in mass from the electron to the tau.

Unlike all three generations of leptons, neither the proton nor neutron are truly fundamental and are composed of even smaller particles called *quarks*. Like leptons, quarks exist in three generations of particles that increase by mass (shown in Table 1.2). However, each generation contains two particles, each carrying a fractional electric charge of either +2/3 or -1/3. While fractions of an elementary charge do not exist freely in nature, quarks are only found in bound states of two or more with a combined integer charge.

Any particle composed of quarks is classified as a *hadron* (from the Greek meaning "heavy"). Hadrons that are made of two quarks are known as *mesons*, which we will discuss when we explore the fundamental forces. Particles containing three quarks, most notably the proton and neutron, are called *baryons*. All protons and neutrons, for instance, consist of light first-generation "up" and "down" quarks. Protons consist of two up quarks and one down quark (UUD), neutrons are composed of two down quarks and one up quark (DDU). The combined fractional charges of the proton equal the measured +1 charge of the proton (2/3 + 2/3 + -1/3 = +1). This works the same for the net zero charge of the neutron. Containing a greater number of slightly more massive down quarks is also what allows the neutron to be slightly heavier than the proton.

Quarks

Flavor	Symbol	Mass	Charge
Up	U	1.7 – 3.3 MeV	+2/3
Down	D	4.5 – 5.3 MeV	-1/3

Charm	C	1,270 MeV	+2/3
Strange	S	101 MeV	-1/3
Top	T	172 GeV	+2/3
Bottom	B	4.18 GeV	-1/3

TABLE 1.2 Six unique "flavors" of quarks are paired by their properties into three generations, which like leptons increase by mass. Middleweight C and S and heavyweight B and T quarks rapidly decay into the first-generation up and down quarks that comprise matter.

Like the muon and tau, the additional mass of later generations of quarks also means proportionally shorter lifetimes before decaying into lighter generations. For this reason, the stable matter in our universe consists overwhelmingly of first-generation up and down quarks.

Beta decay and the neutrino

We have seen that an imbalance of particles can cause atomic nuclei to become unstable, causing them to undergo radioactive decay to achieve a more stable configuration. Radioactive nuclei can gain stability through three primary methods of decay, known as alpha, beta and gamma. Observations of beta decay led to the discovery of the first subatomic particle beyond the atomic nucleus and electrons.

In beta decay one of the neutrons of an unstable nuclei is spontaneously transformed into a proton, and the slight difference in mass is emitted in the form of a high-energy electron, called a beta particle. However, the combined energy of the neutron and beta particle alone, which can be carefully measured, is not quite enough to account for the complete energy in the decay.

To preserve the sacred conservation of energy, physicist Wolfgang Pauli predicted the existence of a yet undiscovered particle emitted in addition to the beta particle. To properly explain observations of beta decay, the particle would have to be far less massive than even the electron, and carry no electric charge, later earning it the accurate name, *neutrino*, Italian for "little neutral one." These properties would also make detecting a neutrino extremely challenging since they would have almost no way to interact with other matter. For this reason, it took almost three decades for the first neutrino to be detected experimentally.

Today, we know neutrinos are created when atomic nuclei are either broken apart, as in the process of beta decay, or forced together as during nuclear processes that occur in the core of the sun or nuclear reactors. In all cases, neutrinos only interact with other particles through the weak nuclear force, which we will explore in chapter three. Despite interacting with virtually nothing after being produced, neutrinos are the most abundant particle in the universe. At any given second 100 trillion neutrinos pass safely through your body as though it were not even there.

Along with the electron, muon and tau, neutrinos belonging to the lepton family are fundamental and structureless particles that also come in three generations. Each generation of neutrino shares similar properties but increases by mass and is closely associated with a charged lepton, either the electron, muon or tau, which is produced during rare interactions between the neutrino and other matter. In this way, each generation of neutrino is said to have an associated lepton *flavor*.

Neutrino flavors

Neutrino flavor	Symbol	Mass
Electron neutrino	V_e	0.02 eV — 0.8 eV
Muon neutrino	V_μ	< 0.19 MeV
Tau neutrino	V_τ	< 18.2 MeV

TABLE 1.3 Three generations of neutrinos, each of which has a lepton-flavor and is closely associated with either the electron, muon or tau particle.

Even today, the exact mass of each neutrino flavor remains unknown, though experimental evidence indicates an electron neutrino weighs somewhere between 0.02 and 0.8 eV, roughly 500,000[th] the mass of an electron. While the masses of the muon- and tau neutrino are currently known with far less precision, they are believed to be less than 0.19 MeV and 18.2 MeV, respectively.

Antimatter

In the 1930s while perfecting the modern description of the atom, in particular the electron, physicists were faced with an unexpected scenario. As sometimes is the case, their modern equations also allowed for a second possible solution, which seemed to describe a particle identical in every way to the electron only with a positive electric charge. Unbeknownst to physicists at the time, the equations were correctly predicting the existence of antimatter, an alternate version of all elementary particles that is identical in all regards but carries an electric charge of the opposite sign. Only two years later, the anti-electron, or *positron* as it is now called, was confirmed experimentally.

Today we know every elementary particle has its own associated antimatter twin; there exist anti-neutrinos, anti-quarks and even composites of anti-protons and anti-neutrons. Further, when a particle and its associated anti-particle collide, they undergo annihilation, and their mass is converted into pure energy as governed by the laws of special relativity and $E = mc2$. The annihilation of matter and antimatter also has practical applications, namely in medicine. Positron Emission Tomography, or a PET scan, relies on positrons encountering the electrons in ordinary matter and annihilating so the resulting energy that is radiated can be detected and used to produce high-resolution images of the body and its internal organs. The antimatter counterparts of elementary particles will continue to play a significant role in our understanding of matter and fundamental forces.

This raises an intriguing question: why do we live in our material world? Our universe is filled with stars, planets, people and other ordinary matter, and very little antimatter by comparison. However, the exact reason for this large disparity is still unknown and our modern theories of cosmology tell us confidently that equal amounts of matter and antimatter should have been created fractions of a second after the Big Bang. Understanding how matter (thankfully) won out over antimatter during the initial moments of the universe is among the leading topics of research in modern particle physics.

Elementary Particles of Matter

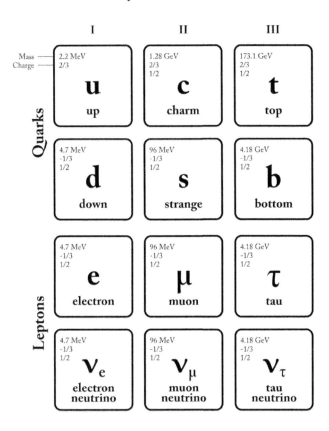

Quantum mechanics

The laws governing the motions and behaviors of atoms and particles

Mechanics is the grand scientific framework governing all matter and energy and the relationship between forces, matter and motion. The laws of classical mechanics were formulated by Galileo, Newton and many others over several centuries and describe the motions of the ordinary objects in our everyday world, from pebbles to trains to planets. These classical laws of nature still serve as the backbone of all modern engineering, spaceflight and even the design and construction of particle detectors and accelerators. However, at the scales of atoms and particles, our predictable and intuitive everyday world resolves into the grainy and uncertain world of quantum mechanics. Though both classical and quantum mechanics provide an extremely well-tested and accurate description of nature in terms of matter and energy, their core principles are almost entirely different and even counterintuitive to one another.

I CLASSICAL MECHANICS

Motion

Objects in our everyday world all have definite and measurable properties, like position, speed and direction, which allow us to determine their exact state of motion. Every object moves in predictable a manner governed by the three fundamental laws of motion, formulated over three hundred years ago by Isaac Newton, which describe how matter moves under the influence of forces:

> *First law (law of inertia): An object at rest remains at rest, and an object in motion remains in motion at constant speed and in a straight line unless acted on by an unbalanced force.*

Inertia is the natural tendency of every physical object to resist change to its state of motion and is why your body wants to continue moving forward even though the car has come to an abrupt stop. Even the ultra-tiny masses of atoms and subatomic particles possess inertia and therefore resist change to their motion.

> *Second law: The acceleration of an object depends on the mass of the object and the amount of force applied.*

The second law describes the relationship between forces and motion and is why the acceleration of a soccer ball increases the harder it is kicked.

Third law: for every action in nature there is an equal and opposite reaction.

Finally, the third law shows us that whenever any physical object exerts a force on another object, the second object will exert a force back that is perfectly equal in its magnitude but in the opposite direction. The third law is at work every time your flight takes off as the wings of the airplane push down on the air and receive an equal upward force in return, lifting the plane into the sky.

Objects in motion can also be described by certain properties, like their energy and momentum. Most importantly, these quantities are also conserved, meaning they can neither be created nor destroyed in nature. This also means that while they may change form or be transferred, their net amount remains constant over time for any physical system.

Consider a simple physical system consisting of two objects, a rolling ball and a stationary ball. The mass of the first ball rolls in a particular direction with a certain amount of kinetic energy (energy of motion) and momentum (its "oomph"), whereas the stationary ball sits at rest with no kinetic energy and no momentum. Upon colliding, some of the energy and momentum from the rolling ball is transferred to the stationary ball, giving it the kinetic energy to move at a certain velocity in the opposite direction of the first ball. The first ball also recoils in the opposite direction and moves at a reduced speed having lost some of its kinetic energy. While both the energy and momentum of the balls is changed and transferred between the two objects, the total amount involved remains perfectly constant and balanced.

Conservation applies not only to linear momentum occurring in straight lines, but also to angular momentum, the rotation of mass around a central axis. The classic example is a figure skater rotating more rapidly as they draw their arms near their body. Upon reducing how spread out their rotating mass is, the skater's body must increase its velocity to ensure their overall angular momentum remains constant.

The many conservation laws that arise in nature will continue to play an important part in our overall journey.

Waves

As opposed to solid material objects with localized properties, some aspects of nature exhibit inherently spread-out and wavelike qualities. All waves are disturbances propagating through a medium and, unlike particles, do not have a single definite position or momentum simply because they naturally exist at many locations and propagate in all directions. Every type of wave can be characterized by the same basic properties:

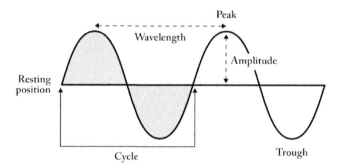

2.1 All waves contain repeating peaks and troughs and can be described by their wavelength, frequency and amplitude.

Wavelength: the distance between any one peak (highest point) to the next, or equivalently, and trough (lowest point) to the next. From a peak, into a trough and back again constitutes one complete cycle of a wave.

Frequency: the measure of how rapidly a wave is oscillating that is determined by the number of peaks that pass by a specific point within a given time. Wavelength and frequency are inversely proportional in that the longer the wavelength the lower the frequency and vice versa.

Amplitude: the maximum point of displacement of the wave from its resting point, the horizontal line running through the middle of the wave. Amplitude is a measure of the strength of a wave, like a tsunami rising high above sea level.

Waves can also interact with matter and themselves in different ways than particles. Namely, they can diffract and spread out when passing through a narrow aperture or bend around an intervening obstacle, the way a stream gracefully curves around a log. When a wave passes through two different mediums, it can change speed and direction, causing it to bend or refract, like the light waves reflecting off a spoon in a glass of water making it appear bent. Waves can even overlap and interact with each other to produce unique and distinct patterns, like the overlapping ripples from dropping two stones in an otherwise still pool of water.

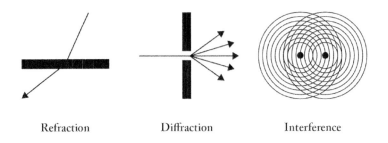

Refraction   Diffraction   Interference

2.2 Waves undergo unique phenomena such as refraction, diffraction and interference.

II QUANTUM MECHANICS

Wave-particle duality

Central to all quantum mechanics is the ability of all matter and energy to exhibit the properties and behaviors of both a particle and a wave, depending on the nature of the experimental methods being employed. This dual behavior was first observed in light, which classically is described as disturbances in electric and magnetic fields radiating out in all directions as continuous waves of electromagnetic energy.

However, at the turn of the twentieth century physicists discovered that light could be equally well described as a stream of discrete individual packets or "quanta" of electromagnetic energy, which were later named *photons*. Specifically, as opposed to a smooth and continuous wave of energy, light consists of discrete individual particles, each of which is restricted to carrying a specific amount energy that is related to the total frequency of the light wave and can be expressed by the following formula:

$$E = hf$$

Where E is the energy of any given individual photon, f is the frequency of the light (sometimes symbolized v) and h is a new constant in nature, known as *Planck's constant* after its original discoverer, and is equal to $6.62607015 \times 10^{-34}$ joule seconds. Understanding the exact value or units of h is not necessary, the importance lies in that it represents the ultra-small scale at which a full wave of continuous energy, like light, is reduced to its smallest most fundamental individual bits.

Most importantly, by assuming that energy at the fundamental level can only exist in amounts that are integer multiples of h, the energy of any physical system is thereby restricted to only taking on specific allowed values. In this way, energy has been *quantized*.

The quantization of energy was also an important step toward a more modern and accurate atomic model. A major problem with our classical solar-system-like understanding of the atom was that any rotating electric charge in nature radiates energy as it accelerates around the curves. As a result, electrons should rapidly expend their energy and go careening into the nucleus in fractions of a single second, rendering the stable matter in our universe impossible.

By quantizing energy electrons are restricted to only existing at specific allowed and stable energy levels simply because anywhere in between is prohibited by the laws of quantum mechanics. Only by absorbing or emitting specific amounts of energy determined by Planck's constant can an electron move to a different energy level. By absorbing a photon of a certain energy, for example, an electron on the innermost level can gain just the right amount energy to move instantaneously to the next highest level. Alternatively, an electron at a higher energy level moves to a lower and more stable level by emitting a photon of just the right energy that is equal to the difference between the two levels. This transitioning of electrons between the energy levels of an atom is the origin of the phrase "quantum leap."

Daring as this new particle model of energy may have been in the early 1900s, it provided highly accurate descriptions and answers to experimental results left unexplained by a pure wave theory of light. Depending on the circumstances under which it is observed, light behaves as both a wave and a particle.

This wave-particle duality is not limited to light or energy but is an inherent property of all matter and energy in the universe, meaning that the particle-like building blocks of matter, like the electron, also exhibit wavelike properties. In fact, even macroscopic objects like your human body can be described by their wavy qualities, only, mathematically we find that the associated wavelength of any even remotely sizable object are themselves far too small to be directly observable, let alone noticeable in everyday life. At atomic and subatomic scales, on the other hand, these matter-waves become unavoidable and must therefore be factored into our overall description of matter.

Double-slit experiment

A classic direct demonstration of this wave-particle duality of matter is in the double-slit experiment where a beam of electrons is fired at a barrier with two tiny parallel slits in the center, and the resulting pattern is observed on a detector screen beyond the barrier. If electrons were entirely particle-like, they would behave in the same manner as balls being thrown at a wall, either colliding with the barrier and being deflected, or passing through one slit or the other. The resulting pattern would be two large stripes where the electrons that passed through one of the slits lands on the detector screen, producing a tiny blip of light.

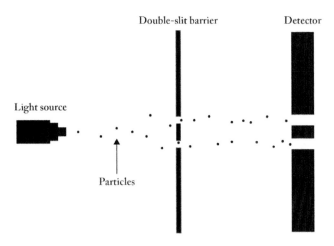

2.3 Electrons and other particles used in the double-slit would be expected to either collide with the solid barrier or pass through one of the slits.

Otherwise, if you performed the same experiment with water would produce completely different results. As the single wave of water collides with the barrier, some flows through each slit, splitting the single wave into two separate waves that expand out from each slit and overlap with each other. Places where the peaks from both waves intersect combine and reinforce into a single even higher peak, whereas a peak from one wave and a trough from the other will intersect and work to reduce or cancel each other out entirely. This combining and cancelling produces a distinct interference pattern of alternating dark and bright stripes on the detector, resembling a crosswalk. Interference patterns are the undeniable mark of wavelike phenomena and are the direct result of the inherently up-and-down nature of all waves.

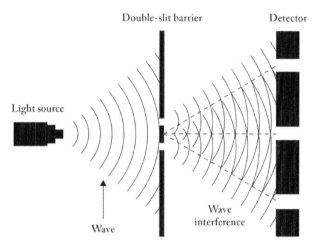

2.4 Wavelike behavior causes the waves to overlap and produce a distinct interference pattern.

Oddly, this is also the same pattern produced when a beam of electrons interacts with the slits; the solid particle-like building blocks of matter produce a pattern only possible from wavelike materials. Further, modern scientific equipment allows for the incoming beam to be throttled so only a single electron is sent through the experiment at a time. Initially, each lone electron behaves in the expected classical particle-like manner, passing through one of the slits and landing randomly in a single localized point on the detector. However, as more electrons are sent through over time, the seemingly random landing place of each individual particle gradually builds up to produce the same wave interference pattern, indicating that each electron passes simultaneously through both slits and overlaps with itself to produce a wave interference pattern.

Finally, by placing additional detectors at the barrier to determine precisely which slit the electron passes through, the wave interference pattern vanishes, and the electrons revert to their classical particle-like behavior of passing through only one slit or the other and producing two bright stripes on the detector. Remove the additional detectors and the wavelike behaviors and interference pattern both return.

Probabilistic motion and the wavefunction

How do we go about describing this dualistic nature of all matter in which subatomic objects like electrons exhibit the properties of both particles and waves? Just as classical everyday objects can be described by their properties and state of motion, subatomic objects can be described by their quantum state, which contains all the relevant information that we can know about it at any given moment, such as its position, momentum, rotation and more. However, the wavelike properties of all quantum objects make it impossible to determine their precise position and momentum simultaneously. To see why, think about ocean waves, for example, where you might know which direction are headed as they come crashing onto the shore, but you have virtually no knowledge of where the wave is located simply because it is naturally spread out over many points. On the other hand, if you zoom in closely to determine the exact position of part of the wave, you no longer retain the information about its momentum because the wave is heading in all directions from the point of observation.

The dualistic state of a quantum object must therefore be described probabilistically by a mathematical function known as a wavefunction, denoted by the Greek symbol Psi, Ψ. As with classical objects, the information about an object and its wavefunction can then be used to predict the state of a particle at a future time. However, unlike the exact and deterministic outcomes of classical mechanics, the wavefunction provides a probabilistic prediction of a quantum object's motion.

Quantum wave equations like the Schrödinger or Dirac equation can be used to determine how the wavefunction is likely to evolve overtime, and therefore what state it is likely to be in. In the end, solutions to these complex quantum equations trace out the dualistic wavy behavior of discrete particles like the electron. However, the evolution of the wavefunction does not describe the literal physical motion of a particle waving up-and-down through space, but instead provides an abstract distribution of probabilities of all the possible states the particle might exist in at some point in time. Places where the amplitude of the wave is highest indicate the regions of space where a particle is most likely to be located, and places where the wave is lowest indicating regions where a particle is unlikely to be found.

These equations can be solved to determine the likelihood of finding an electron in each state around a nucleus, which can be used to produce a modern quantum model of the atom. Like a map of probabilities wrapped around the nucleus, the probable states and positions of the electron can be predicted with wonderful accuracy and align perfectly with experimental data. Quantum wave equations can even be solved to determine the possible shape, orientation and other properties of electron orbitals around the nucleus.

Yet, the laws of quantum mechanics also tell us that until a particle is measured and observed it must be thought of as existing in a blend or superposition of all possible states at once, like a cloud of all possible outcomes. Only upon determining the position of a particle, say an electron on a detector screen, does its wavefunction "collapse" to a single state. This superposition was demonstrated clearly in the case of the double-slit experiment as the unobserved electrons exist in a superposition of all possible states and outcomes in which they traveled not through only one but both slits, allowing the states to overlap and interfere with one another to produce the wave interference pattern on the detector. Yet, by applying additional detectors at the barrier to observe the electron's exact path, its wavefunction was forced to collapse to a single state of passing through one slit or the other.

While the exact interpretation of how and why the wavefunction collapses as well as the exact nature of our role as the observer remain matters of debate, superposition is important in our understanding the nature of matter at subatomic scales. It also plays a central role in all quantum computing by allowing information ordinarily stored as either 0 or 1 to instead be stored as 0, 1 or a superposition of both 0 and 1, allowing quantum computers to perform tasks that are impossible for classical computers.

Classically speaking, if an object does not possess enough energy, it will be incapable of overcoming certain potential energy barriers. This is what prevents a ball across the floor from being able to mysteriously scale the steps of your staircase or pass through a wall. However, wave-particle duality and the resulting probabilistic nature of matter allow for strange events like these at quantum scales. While the probability distribution provided by the wavefunction indicates places where a particle may be extremely unlikely to be located, no place reduces completely to zero. In other words, while it may be overwhelmingly likely to find an electron orbiting the nucleus of its atom, there is a remarkably small yet non-zero chance that it is instead far outside the bounds of the atom, or millions of miles away, or on the opposite end of the known universe.

As a result of this, we find from the wavefunction of a particle, say an electron, colliding with a solid barrier, for example, there are also less likely but nevertheless non-zero states in which the electron will be found beyond the barrier. Again, while finding the electron in such an unexpected state may prove highly unlikely and decreases exponentially the farther the particle gets from the barrier, it is still within the realm of possibility because of the wave-particle duality of all matter and the laws of quantum mechanics.

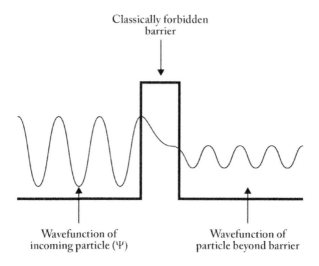

2.5 The duality of matter allows it to *tunnel* through classically impenetrable barriers, which while exponentially less likely are within the realm of possible events in nature.

The phenomena of quantum tunneling places a critical role in the nuclear processes in our sun, allowing the nuclei of hydrogen atoms to overcome otherwise impenetrable forces to fuse into heavier elements that fuel and power our star. The ability for matter to overcome impenetrable energy barriers is also what allows for particles to be spontaneously created and emitted during many radioactive decay processes, which we will explore in future chapters.

Uncertainty principle

Unlike in the case of classical mechanics, the uncertainties in the properties and states of subatomic objects are not merely limitations of our measuring tools or technological capabilities but a direct result of wave-particle duality. As we know already, the properties of particles and waves are entirely different from one another and impose natural limits on how well we can determine both simultaneously. These natural limits are governed by the uncertainty principle, which states that the more precisely we determine one property, the less precisely we can determine another, and can be expressed as:

$$\Delta_x \Delta_p \geq \frac{h}{4\pi}$$

Importantly, the uncertainty principle does not apply to all properties but only specific pairs of interrelated or conjugate properties, such as position and momentum. The principle also does not imply that we cannot determine the position or momentum of a particle with terrific precision, only that we cannot precisely determine both simultaneously and that decreasing our uncertainty in one property necessarily increases our uncertainty in the other. This same relationship also exists for other pairs of properties, such as energy and time, that will become important as we discuss the fundamental forces in later chapters.

Spin and the Pauli exclusion principle

In addition to their linear motion, quantum objects also have the property of angular momentum, or quantum *spin*, which is completely different than our familiar ideas of rotation or spinning.

To start, particles like electrons exhibit similar magnetic effects and properties to a spinning electrically charged object. However, calculations show that to produce the measured effects the electron would have to be rotating faster than the speed of light, which is impossible, or have a diameter far larger than the atom itself, which is clearly not correct. Instead, all particles possess an intrinsic amount of angular momentum without physically rotating.

Further, the intrinsic spin of a particle, unlike that of a figure skater or rotating ball, never changes speed or direction. All particles spin at an identical rate in the same direction for their entire existence. And unlike the continuous uninterrupted rotation of ordinary classical objects, particle spin is restricted to only taking on certain values determined by Planck's constant, meaning spin, like energy, is a quantized quantity in nature. However, it turns out that instead of integer multiples of Planck's constant, the spin of electrons only occurs in intervals equal to half of one fundamental unit. All electrons, we say, are "spin-half."

Even more unintuitive to our familiar notion of rotation, the spin of electrons can only occur in two possible orientations, either clockwise or counterclockwise, which are arbitrarily labeled *spin up* and *spin down*. Therefore, any given electron in the universe can only occupy one of two possible spin states, either +1/2 or -1/2, depending on which direction it is rotating. All particles with a half unit of spin are classified as *Fermions*.

This intrinsic angular momentum turns out to be a deep fundamental property of nature and carries significant implications on the structure of matter. A fundamental principle in quantum mechanics, known as the *exclusion principle*, states that no two Fermions can occupy the same quantum state, meaning no two can possess identical properties, including their orientation of spin. To state this more simply, no two Fermions can be at the exact place at the exact same time in nature.

Imagine a simple hydrogen atom in which an electron orbits stably around a single-proton nucleus at the lowest and innermost energy level. Beyond this, the next stable configuration, a helium atom, would be two electrons on the lowest energy level around a nucleus of two protons and two neutrons. While their mass, electric charge and other properties are identical, nothing prevents a second electron from also occupying the same energy level, so long as its spin is oriented in the opposite direction of the other electron, thereby allowing the two particles to exist in two unique quantum states.

Now, what if we add a third electron to the atom to make lithium? The first energy level is now completely occupied by two electrons whose states differ only by their orientation of spin. The laws of quantum mechanics prohibit an additional electron from occupying the same energy level simply because it would necessarily have to be either spin up or spin down and occupy an identical quantum state to one of the other two electrons. Instead, the third electron must occupy the next highest energy level, which itself can contain a finite number of electrons. In this way, the intrinsic spin of particles is responsible for the orbital structure of matter and therefore all of chemistry as well.

Forces

The fundamental interactions between particles

A surprisingly small handful of particles constitute the fundamental building blocks of all the matter we see around us. Similarly, every push, pull, combination or division of matter in the universe can be attributed to just four fundamental forces. Namely gravity, electromagnetism and the strong and weak nuclear forces.

Gravity dominates over cosmological distances and dictates the large-scale structure of the universe. However, with a relative strength that is 10^{36} times weaker than electromagnetism, the effects of gravity are virtually nonexistent among the microscopic structure of the atom and can be essentially ignored.

Electromagnetism, as we already know, arises from forces between charges and is responsible for light. Like gravity, electromagnetism also acts across universal scales which is how we can see the light from ancient and distant galaxies. The laws of electromagnetism are the origin of the axiom that opposite charges attract and like charges repel, which is the reason the equal but opposite electric charge keeps electrons bound firmly to the nucleus and defines the atomic structure. The same electromagnetic forces are also responsible for our very ability to perceive matter in the first place. Between the tiny central nucleus and surrounding electron shells lies nothing, rendering well over 99.99% of all atoms completely empty space. Were it not for the powerful electric and magnetic fields permeating this space, holding this book in your hands, lying on top of a bed, or any other physical action would be impossible because atoms would simply pass right through one another.

The same electromagnetic laws should also apply to the identical positive charges of protons, causing all atomic nuclei to spontaneously blast apart. At a hundred times more powerful than electromagnetism, the strong force easily overcomes this electric repulsion to ensure protons and neutrons remain tightly bound in the nucleus. However, being composite particles, the binding of protons and neutrons together in the nucleus itself proves to be a secondary effect or *residual force* arising from an even more fundamental strong force acting between constituent quarks. The powerful bond between up and down quarks provides the fundamental stability of hadrons like protons and neutrons, and therefore all the matter with which we interact and are made from.

Unlike gravity or electromagnetism, the strong force acts only over the tiny distance of the atomic nucleus, approximately 10^{-15} meters. Because of this, protons and neutrons must be in extremely close proximity before the effects of the strong force can overcome their mutual repulsion. This occurs in the hot and dense cores of stars where atoms of hydrogen are smashed together with enough energy to bind and form more massive helium nuclei, giving off excess energy in the process. This is the nuclear process that powers every star in the universe, including our sun.

Finally, the weak nuclear force is responsible for the radioactive decay of atomic nuclei. Specifically, the weak force is responsible for beta decay in which one of the neutrons in an unstable nucleus, such as an isotope, is transformed into a proton, shedding the additional energy in the form of emitted particles. By transforming a neutron into a proton, the chemical identity of the atom is also changed in the process, which seems like a rather dramatic force. The term "weak" instead refers to the fact that the force only acts over the tiny distances of 10^{-18} m, confining its effects to within individual nucleons and making it by far the shortest range of any fundamental force in nature.

Quantum field theory

The concept of the field has been an integral part of all physics for many centuries, originally used to describe the effects of gravity and electromagnetism reaching invisibly across space. The gravitational field caused by the mass of Earth, for instance, permeates hundreds of thousands of miles of surrounding space to keep the moon securely in its orbit. Electric fields reach across the vast emptiness of the atomic structure to keep protons and electrons bound. In this way, we classically imagine fields as arising from forces.

In quantum mechanics, this order is reversed so that the field becomes truly fundamental, giving rise to the many aspects of nature. All quantum fields permeate the entire universe, existing at every point in space and time, however, they differ considerably from our classical idea of fields. ***Quantum field theory*** (QFT), first developed in the 1930s, applies the laws and principles of quantum mechanics to the classical concept of the field, including quantizing the field itself. Like energy, momentum and several other quantities in classical physics, the values of a classical field occur continuously and smoothly from one point to the next. By applying the laws of quantum mechanics, the state of the field itself at any given point is restricted to certain allowed values, it is quantized.

Within the framework of quantum field theory, the building blocks of matter themselves are considered as tiny waves or excitations of an even more fundamental field. When localized to extremely small regions of space, these quantum excitations can be interpreted as particles in our more familiar sense. Quantum field theory views all elementary particles in nature as an excitation of its own associated underlying quantum field. Electrons, for instance, are excited quantum states of a fundamental electron field, quarks are excitations of a quarks field, and so on.

Like particles themselves, quantum fields can also interact with one another. In this way, energy from one field can be transferred into another field, giving rise to excitations. And given that energy itself is quantized, so too are the particular energy levels of any given field. The electron field, as an example, only occurs or exists in states that are exact integer multiples of 0.511 MeV and nothing in between.

We imagine classical fields like a lake sitting placidly, waiting for some type of disturbance to cause it to wave and ripple; a charged object producing disturbances in the electric field, for example. Quantum fields, on the other hand, are roiling with activity, even in the absence of any disturbances. The laws of quantum mechanics, namely the uncertainty principle, demand that every field have associated with them a specific minimum amount of energy, meaning that the energy of the field must always be some non-zero value. As a result, all quantum fields undergo vacuum fluctuations, whereby the non-zero energy of the field allows for pairs of virtual particles to be continually produced and annihilated.

More specifically, by producing a particle with energy, momentum and electric charge, the field must also produce an associated antiparticle to conserve electric charge. Neither the energy or momenta of the virtual particles are strictly conserved but are transferred back into the field as the particle and antiparticle annihilate within extremely short times determined by the uncertainty principle. In this, no quantum field is ever truly in a state of rest and vacuum fluctuations of virtual particle-antiparticle pairs are constantly bursting in and out of existence throughout every field everywhere in the universe all the time.

Quantum field theory also provides a quantum mechanical interpretation of the fundamental interactions in nature is through the exchange of force carrying particles, one of which we have already encountered, the photon, transmitter of the electromagnetic force. Instead of a continuous electric and magnetic mist permeating otherwise empty space between charged objects, we can interpret all electromagnetic interactions as the constant exchange of photons. Imagine, for instance, two electrons approaching one another. As they grow near both electrons emit and absorb a constant flurry of photons that transmit repulsive electric forces, causing the particles to fly apart. As depicted in diagram 3.1, the energy from each emitted photon causes the electron (left solid line) to experience a slight recoil, almost like tossing a heavy ball. As the photon (wavy line) travels through space and is absorbed, its energy causes the other electron (right solid line) to experience a recoil of equal magnitude but in the opposite direction.

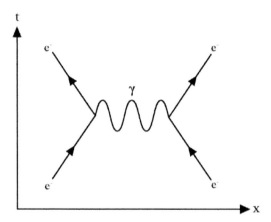

3.1 An electromagnetic interaction between two electrons as depicted through the exchange of a photon. Specifically, the incoming electron (left) emits a photon (γ) causing it to recoil slightly. A second nearby electron (right) then absorbs the emitted photon, also experiencing a slight recoil. This photon exchange is the mechanism transmitting the repulsive electric force experienced between the electrons.

There are a theoretically infinite number of ways all the elementary particles of nature can interact with each other through the fundamental forces. In all cases, the same conservation laws of classical mechanics are still upheld and must remain constant throughout all particle interactions. These conservation laws a crucial tool for predicting the outcomes of the many complex particle interactions in the universe:

Mass-energy: Albert Einstein's special theory of relativity demands that both the mass and energy of the particles involved will be the same prior to and after all interactions.

Charge: electric charge is also conserved through all interactions.

Momentum: the product of the involved particles' masses and velocities must also remain intact under all circumstances.

Depending on the type of interaction and particles involved, other properties may also be conserved. The violation of these conservation values will also prove particularly important.

Photons themselves, though they are the carrier of the electromagnetic force, are electrically neutral. Also, centuries of experimental evidence and measurements indicate that the photon has no mass, which means there is nothing less massive and more stable for it decay into. Though, in certain interactions, such as ***pair production***, photons can interact with an electric field to temporarily produce matter-antimatter pairs of an electron and positron, which rapidly annihilate to produce two photons (pure energy).

In addition to electromagnetism and the photon, both nuclear interactions can also be interpreted as being mediated by the exchange of their own unique force carrying particles. The strong nuclear interaction is mediated by the ***gluon***, which as its name insinuates is the particle that binds quarks firmly together to form hadrons like protons and neutrons. Across slightly greater distances a type of particle known as the ***meson*** mediates the residual strong interaction that binds entire protons and neutrons together in the nucleus.

The weak nuclear interaction is mediated by three potential force carrying particles, known as the W^+, W^- and Z^0. Last, even gravitational interactions are theorized to be mediated by the exchange of the hypothetical *graviton*, which has no mass or charge.

In the last chapter we were introduced to quantum spin, the intrinsic angular momentum possessed by all particles. We found that the elementary particles of matter are classified as fermions, which all possess a half unit of spin. Most importantly, we found that all fermions must obey the Pauli exclusion principle, meaning no two spin-half particles can exist in an identical quantum state, they cannot be in the exact same place at the same time.

To the contrary, force carrying particles in nature all possess integer spin values of either 1 or 0 and comprise a class of particles known as *bosons*. Unlike fermions, bosons are not subject to the uncertainty principle and are entirely free — and even prefer — to share identical quantum states. In other words, multiple bosons can be in the same place at the same time, which makes sense considering they mediate forces and their associated strengths.

Fundamental interactions

Force	Boson	Mass	Charge	Spin
Electromagnetism	Photon	0	0	1
Strong Interaction	Gluon	0	0	1
Weak Interaction	W$^+$, W$^-$	80.377 GeV/c^2	±1 e	1
	Z^0	91.187 GeV/c^2	0	1
Gravity	Graviton	0	0	1

TABLE 3.1 Each of the fundamental interactions of nature is mediated through the exchange of its own specific force-carrying boson. All exchange particles are massless and have zero electric charge except for the W and Z bosons that mediate weak interactions.

Both photons and gluon, carriers of electromagnetism and the strong nuclear interaction, are themselves massless particles. The W and Z bosons mediating the weak force, on the other hand, possess relatively huge masses, roughly 80 and 91 times the mass of a proton, respectively. This raises an immediate question of how particles, with real physical properties like mass and energy, can be produced out of seemingly nowhere without violating one of the most sacred laws in nature. The conservation of energy clearly states that both the beginning and final amount of energy contained in any system, be it a particle, field or anything else, must always be perfectly equal. In short, it is impossible to make something out of nothing. How can a neutron, with a mass of 941 MeV/c^2, spontaneously create and emit a particle like a W boson, which itself is over 80 times as massive as the neutron?

Recall from our discussions about quantum mechanics in chapter one the Heisenberg uncertainty principle, which is the mathematical relationship between position and momentum that automatically prevents either property from being determined simultaneously with perfect certainty. This deeply rooted uncertainty in nature is why it is impossible to determine the exact position of an electron around the nucleus of an atom. The same relationship also exists between energy and time, which can be formulated as:

$$\Delta E \Delta t \geq h/4\pi$$

Only now, we find the resulting uncertainties allow for conservation laws to be violated and energy to be borrowed directly from a field itself, but only for proportionally short amounts of time determined by Planck's constant. Energy borrowed through this loophole is how exchange particles can be constantly created, emitted and reabsorbed to mediate interactions.

However, nothing in nature can travel faster than the speed of light, meaning that even force carrying particles can travel so far during any given time. This mixture of the uncertainty principle and the speed of light therefore dictates the range of the fundamental interactions by limiting particles of larger mass to only traveling extremely short distances before being reabsorbed. The large energies required to create the W and Z particles mediating the weak interaction, for instance, are only able to travel extremely short distances (10^{-18} meters) before having to be reabsorbed to fulfill the uncertainty principle.

The force-carrying particles mediating fundamental interactions under the limits of the Heisenberg uncertainty principle are produced and annihilated in such brief periods of time that they are not directly observable and are therefore referred to as ***virtual particles***. While not observable directly, the effects of virtual particles on other particles can be measured to a high degree of accuracy and plays a critical role in all fundamental interactions.

Feynman diagrams

Returning to our earlier depiction of two electrons interacting through the exchange of photons, we can use the same approach for any type of fundamental interaction. By applying a simple set of rules, a wealth of important information about complicated particle interactions can be reduced to comprehensive visual representations called a Feynman diagram, in which the x-axis represents space (x) and the y-axis time (t).

- Fermions are drawn as solid lines with arrows running in the direction of the time axis.
- Anti-fermions are solid lines with arrows running in the opposite direction of the time axis, or backwards in time.
- Bosons are shown by wavy lines:

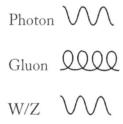

In Feynman diagrams, every vertex (convergence of three lines) represents some type of interaction between particles. It is often helpful to describe the strengths of each of the fundamental interactions relative to one another, which can be accomplished by associating each force with a unique coupling constant, typically denoted α. In this regard, the strength of the strong interaction (α_s) is represented by a coupling constant of 1. Comparatively, electromagnetic interactions are characterized by a coupling constant of 1/137 (α), weak interactions (α_w) 10^{-6} and gravitational interactions (α_g) 10^{-39}. Coupling constants allow us to make useful comparisons between the extremely different fundamental interactions in nature because they are dimensionless quantities, meaning their values are equally valid within all units of measurement.

Most importantly, each vertex must also take into consideration the properties that are conserved in all interactions, which are mass-energy, momentum and electric charge. We can see these conservation laws at work in our example diagram from before showing electrons interacting by exchanging a virtual photon.

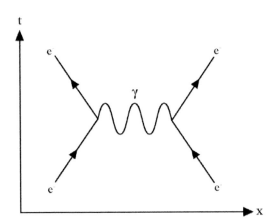

3.2 Feynman diagram describing the forces exerted between two electrons through the exchange of a virtual photon.

By emitting the virtual photon, the incoming electron (left) recoils and loses a tiny amount of its energy. As the photon is absorbed by the receiving electron (right), it also recoils and gains the same amount of energy lost by the first electron, thereby conserving total energy. Further, the limitations of the uncertainty principle allow for the virtual photon's ultra-short existence to go temporarily unnoticed during the exchange (sine wave in the middle).

Momentum is conserved in a similar fashion. As the first electron recoils from emitting the virtual photon it loses a small amount of its momentum shown metaphorically by the shift in the diagram line. The photon then carries the lost momentum away where it gets absorbed by the opposing electron, causing it to gain an equal amount and conserving the total momentum in the interaction.

Finally, since photons themselves are electrically neutral, the -1 e charge of both electrons involved remains unchanged.

Strong nuclear interaction

Living up to its name, the strong force or strong interaction, is by far the strongest of the four fundamental forces at around 137 times the strength of electromagnetism, the second most powerful force. As opposed to gravity and electromagnetism, the strong interaction only acts over remarkably short range of 10-15 meters (roughly the size of the nucleus), we do not experience it directly. However, along with the so-called weak force, the two nuclear interactions are both essential to the structure of matter in the universe. While all the forces share some similarities, the nuclear interactions operate far differently than the more familiar two forces.

Just as electromagnetic interactions arise from the property of electric charge, the strong interaction between quarks arises from a fundamental property called *color charge*, an innate property possessed by all quarks and gluons. However, the strong force involves no visual color in the everyday macroscopic sense, but rather is a rough analogy for the way quarks combine like the three primary colors (red, green and blue) to form colorless or white particles.

In the more technical sense, color is a quantum number with three possible values arbitrarily labeled *red*, *green* and *blue*, with any given quark possessing a charge of one of the three states of color. Since quarks cannot exist freely in nature, neither can individual color charges, requiring them to be in the bound color-neutral, or simply *colorless* state in which we observe matter in our universe. However, because quarks and gluons are the only particles that carry color charge, only hadrons — the particles comprised of two or more quarks — can interact via color charge and the strong force. Hadrons, of course, include baryon particles with three quarks, like protons and neutrons. A proton, for example, may be a bound state of a red up quark, a blue up quark and a green down quark. Alternatively, all generations of antiquarks also possess one of three anti-color states (anti-red, anti-blue or anti-green). Combining a blue up quark and an anti-blue down quark, for instance, produces a type of meson known as the Pi meson, or simply *pion*, which also plays a critical role in the strong force.

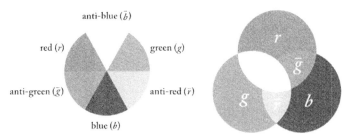

3.3 The strong interactions between quarks occur through the exchange of a three-variable property of color force. Mixing all three "primary" colors or anticolors together produces the neutral or "colorless" matter particles we observe in nature.

The strong-force-carrying gluons themselves also possess color charge, allowing them to interact strongly and exchange color with other quarks, antiquarks and even other gluons. Unlike quarks, gluons carry a combination of two colors, one red, green or blue, as well as one anti-color, anti-red, anti-blue or anti-green. Carrying two colors also allows for many possible color charge configurations for gluons:

Red / anti-red

Red / anti-green

Red / anti-blue

Green / anti-red

Green / anti-green

Green / anti-blue

Blue / anti-red

Blue / anti-green

Blue / anti-blue

In a most basic way, the exchange of color can be imagined as a quark of one color emitting a two-colored gluon that is then absorbed by another quark, thereby changing the color charge of each involved quark. Like the exchange of photons giving rise to electromagnetic interactions, the constant exchange of gluons gives rise to the color field that exists to keep quarks permanently bound into colorless hadrons.

The following diagram is useful for visualizing the exchange of multiple colors by gluons:

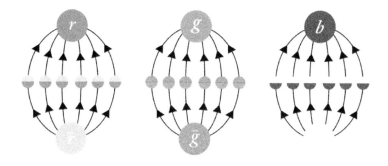

3.4 The force carriers of the strong force, gluons, also carry color force and possess two colors, one color and one anti-color.

Electromagnetism and gravity both follow what is known as an inverse-square law, meaning while their range is infinite, the intensity of the force is inversely proportional to the square of the distance from the source. For instance, if you stand twice as far from a bulb the light will be four times less intense, move four times farther away and the intensity will be 16 times less intense, and so on. This inverse relationship is what allows the intensity of electromagnetic forces to increase as charged particles like protons and electrons come into close contact.

The intensity of the strong interaction between quarks, however, does not obey such a law and its strength does not decrease over distance but remains the same. As a result, as the distance between quarks increases, so does the amount of energy required to overcome the powerful pull of the strong interaction. Ultimately, the amount of energy required to overpower the strong force becomes greater than the amount needed for nature to simply produce a new quark-antiquark pair. This mechanism is what causes quarks to remain permanently confined to bound states of hadrons like protons and neutrons.

However, experimentally, we find that as quarks come into extremely close proximity with one another (as in the boundaries of a hadron), the strength of the interaction reduces. Eventually, the strong force weakens to the point where quarks can move and behave as free particles within the confines of their parent particle, a phenomenon known as asymptotic freedom. The quark model, gluons and color charge are all described by branch of physics known as quantum chromodynamics, or simply QCD, which was developed primarily during the 1970s and is one of the most successful and experimentally precise theories in modern physics.

As we already know, the strong interaction works at two capacities to both bind quarks into hadrons and to bind hadrons like protons and neutrons together in the atomic nucleus. Though both arise from the fundamental strong interactions between constituent quarks, the residual strong force binding protons and neutrons is considerably different from the fundamental strong interaction in many ways.

Not only is the residual force far weaker in strength, it also does decrease in intensity over distance. The residual force is no longer directly mediated by gluons but by mesons, types of hadrons composed of a quark-antiquark pair. While many types of mesons are sufficient for mediating the residual nuclear force, a type of meson known as the pion is often the transmitter between protons and neutrons. Comprised of an up quark and an anti-down quark, Pions are the lightest mesons at roughly 140 MeV/c^2 but are still highly unstable and decay rapidly into lighter particles such as muons and neutrinos. However, their relatively light weight and short lifetime make them ideal for mediating the residual nuclear forces across the tiny distances between protons and neutrons.

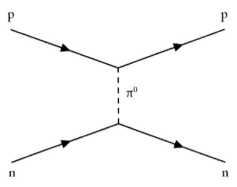

3.5 The residual strong force acting between a proton and neutron through the exchange of a neutral Pi meson, or pion.

Despite still acting over short extremely short nuclear distances and being far weaker than the fundamental strong force, the residual force is still a hundred times stronger than electromagnetism and can easily overcome the repulsive forces between protons. Were the strong interaction only limited to its fundamental ranges between quarks, the formation of stable atomic nuclei and matter as we know it would not be possible. In this way, both capacities of the strong interaction are particularly important in nature.

The importance of the strong force goes far beyond the nucleus. The dense and high-energy conditions in the cores of stars, including our own sun, causes atoms of the most basic element, hydrogen, to bounce wildly around and collide. As the single-proton nucleus of each hydrogen atom is forced into extremely close contact, the strong interaction kicks in, easily overcoming the proton's mutually repulsive electric forces, and allowing the nuclei to fuse together. and releasing a tremendous amount of energy in the process. The tremendous amount of energy released during this fusion process is the nuclear fuel that powers our sun, warms our planet, allows for the possibility of life. This is possible because the strong forces allow the quarks and hadrons of nuclei tightly bound to endure the fusion process.

Weak nuclear interaction

Despite being considerably weaker than electromagnetism and the strong interaction, the weak nuclear interaction is still far stronger than gravity and plays a critical role in matter. Atomic nuclei are most stable when they contain an equal ratio of protons to neutrons and by being the only force capable of completely transforming the flavor of quarks and therefore the identity of hadrons, like protons or neutrons, the weak interaction is responsible for the overall stability of matter in the universe. However, being mediated by W and Z bosons with relatively huge masses, the weak force is limited to acting only over 10^{-18} meters, giving it by far the shortest range of any force. W bosons themselves carry an electric charge of either +1 e in the case of the W⁺ or -1 e for the W⁻), allowing it to mediate a variety of interactions, from radioactive decay to nuclear fusion in the sun.

The W boson gets its name from the fact that it is the primary mediator of *weak* interactions. Depending on which particle a W boson interacts with it will follow one of three possible decay paths:

Leptonic: in roughly 67% of decays, a W boson will decay into a lepton-antilepton pair, one charged and one neutral, for example an electron and electron antineutrino as in beta-minus decay.

$$W^+ \rightarrow e^+ + \nu_e$$
$$W^- \rightarrow e^- + \nu_e$$

Hadronic: around 33% of decays produce a quark-antiquark pair with complementary -1/3 and +2/3 charges. Most hadronic decays result in first-generation up and down quarks, but rarer decays also produce combinations of all generations and flavors.

$$W^{\pm} \rightarrow q + q$$

Tauonic: far more rarely (roughly 11%), a W boson decays to a tau lepton and antineutrino.

$$W^+ \rightarrow \tau^+ \nu_\tau$$

$$W^- \rightarrow \tau^- \nu_\tau$$

In the case of beta decay, which we were introduced to in chapter one, an additional neutron in an unstable nucleus spontaneously transforms into a proton, electron and antineutrino, which can be symbolized as $n \rightarrow p + e^- + \bar{\nu}_e$. At a more fundamental level, this process is mediated by the emission of either W- or W+ bosons by the individual up or down quarks inside the protons and neutrons, resulting in either beta-minus or beta-plus decay. In a beta-minus decay, one of the down quarks in a neutron emits a W-, causing its electric charge to charge from -1/3 to +2/3, thereby changing its flavor from down to up in the process. As a result, what was once a neutron now contains just one down quark and two up quarks, making it a proton and allowing the nucleus to gain stability. Because of the uncertainty principle, the massive W- then travels a very short distance before decaying into an electron and antineutrino. Alternatively, an unstable nucleus with too many protons may undergo a similar decay process, instead emitting a W+ which then decays into a positron and regular neutrino, or $p \rightarrow n + e^+ + V_e$.

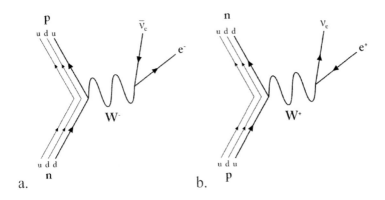

3.6 In beta-minus decay a down quark emits a W-, which travels a short distance before decaying into an electron and an antineutrino. During beta-plus decay, a W+ is emitted and rapidly decays into a regular neutrino and a positron. In all cases, the emission of a W boson changes both the electric charge and therefore flavor of the interacting quarks.

Both forms of beta decay have many practical applications. The emission of positrons through beta-plus decay is used in PET scanning (Positron Emission Tomography), which uses three-dimensional imaging of the body's interior to diagnose and monitor many critical diseases. Many effective cancer treatments also rely on the beta decay processes resulting from radioactive nuclei. Another example is the decay of carbon, the element central to all living organisms. In particular, the isotope carbon-14 contains six protons and eight neutrons, making its nucleus unstable enough to undergo beta-minus decay into nitrogen-14 (seven protons and seven neutrons). By measuring the remaining carbon-14 atoms in the tissue of ancient organisms, scientists can very accurately determine their ages. This type of radiocarbon dating has become a critical tool for studying the evolution of species, ancient archaeology, and more, and is possible because of the underlying weak nuclear interactions in nature.

The weak interaction also plays a critical role in the nuclear fusion that powers every star, including our sun. We have already discussed how the strong interaction allows protons to collide and overcome their repulsive electric forces to fuse into heavier nuclei. Most commonly, hydrogen nuclei of one proton are fused together to ultimately form heavier helium nuclei. In order for this to occur, one of the two colliding protons must transform into a neutron. This transformation is mediated through the exchange of a W^+, which then rapidly decays into a positron and a neutrino (you might recognize this as the beta-plus decay process discussed previously). The proton and neutron can now fuse into the heavier hydrogen isotope of deuterium, which are then able to quickly fuse into fully stable helium nuclei of two protons and two neutrons. While the energy of the strong interaction allows for the fusion of nuclei together, it is the weak interaction that allows one of the protons to transform into a neutron, thereby undergoing decay to achieve more stable nuclear configurations. In this way both the strong and weak nuclear interactions work together to allow the fusion processes that fuel our star and allow for life on our planet.

The charged interactions mediated by the W^- and W^+ are considered weak charged currents. However, the third carrier of the weak force, the Z^0, mediates so-called weak *neutral* current interactions. As the final missing particle in our modern model of particle physics, the Z was named symbolically of the last letter in the English alphabet.

While the W boson is the primary mediator of weak interactions, the Z^0 is no less important and without it, neutrinos could not interact at all, even among themselves. Since neutrinos carry no color charge they cannot interact strongly through the exchange of gluons, nor can they interact electrically by exchanging photons. The only way for neutrinos to interact with each other or matter at all is through weak neutral current interactions mediated by Z bosons. As we have just seen in the processes of beta plus and beta minus decay, for example, W bosons mediate the transformation of a neutron into a proton, which then rapidly decays into an electron and antineutrino. However, the resulting beta decay products (either the electron and antineutrino or positron and neutrino) also undergo their own weak interactions which are mediated by the Z^0.

Being electrically neutral, any weak interactions mediated by the Z^0 are considered weak neutral currents and allow both the charge and therefore flavor of interacting particles to remain unchanged. And because it carries zero electric or color charge, the net charge of Z boson decay products must also be zero to conserve charge. There are many possible decay paths for the Z^0, including:

Leptonic: roughly 10% of Z decays produce a charged lepton-antilepton pair, with roughly equal chances of being an electron-positron, muon-antimuon or tau-antitau.

$$Z \rightarrow l^+ + l^-$$

Hadronic: 70% of decays produce a quark-antiquark pair, one of the many examples of which is a quark flavor and its equivalent anti-flavor:

$$Z \rightarrow u\,\bar{u}$$

$$Z \rightarrow d\,d$$

$$Z \rightarrow c\,c$$

$$Z \rightarrow s\,s$$

$$Z \rightarrow b\,b$$

Neutrino: roughly 20% of the time a Z boson decays into a neutrino-antineutrino pair, making these "invisible" decays extremely difficult to detect.

The different quark and lepton flavors allow for 24 possible decay paths for the Z^0, all in all. Z bosons (as well as W bosons) are also produced as decay products of extremely high-energy processes, such as the annihilation of electron-positron pairs, proton-proton collisions and other processes mostly produced via modern particle accelerators. While neutral current interactions are stronger than gravity, they are far less powerful than — and easily obscured by — electromagnetic interactions, making them extremely difficult to detect experimentally. While both the W and Z bosons were first theorized in the 1960s, it took until 1983 for both particles to be detected experimentally.

Particle detectors and accelerators

The experimental means by which we prove our theories

Nobody ever has or ever will observe an atom or subatomic particle directly. Certainly not with their eyes, and not even using the most advanced microscopes. To "see" something requires bouncing light off it, which proves to be impractical for observing subatomic objects. For starters, subatomic particles are dramatically smaller (around $1/10,000^{th}$) than the wavelengths of visible light, making it impossible to "bounce" light off them. Further, as we have learned, the fact that light interacts directly with matter also makes determining its precise properties impossible. Instead, the best we can do is to detect particles indirectly through elaborate experiments and increasingly sophisticated equipment and technology.

Particle detectors come in all types and sizes from crude and shoebox-sized to word class modern experiments like **ATLAS** or **CMS** at the European Center for Nuclear Research (CERN), which each weigh several thousand tons. All particle detectors share the single goal of studying the properties of otherwise invisible elementary particles by observing their indirect effects on visible matter.

Early versions of detectors relied on the ability of charged particles to ionize matter, meaning its atoms lose one or many electrons. This can be accomplished by either:

- Knocking electrons completely free from their atoms creates a detectable trail of ionized atoms and electrons.

- Exciting electrons into higher energy orbitals, which settle back into their ground state by emitting detectable scintillations of photons.

Cloud chamber

One of the successful early particle detectors was the cloud chamber, invented in 1911 just over a decade after the only known subatomic particle, the electron, had been discovered. Through the following decades, cloud chambers would be used to confirm the existence of antimatter with the first detection of a positron and would also play a vital role in the discovery of the neutron and the muon, the electron's heavier second-generation lepton cousin.

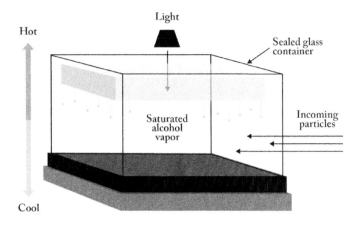

4.1 Cloud chambers use supersaturated alcohol vapors inside a sealed glass container to create visible ion trails left by charged particles as they pass through.

A basic cloud chamber consists of a sealed glass container with a heated upper plate and cooled lower plate. A liquid alcohol such as isopropyl is applied to the warm upper region, which travels downward as it cools, saturating the container with alcohol vapor. Charged particles traveling through the container ionize atoms of gas, which then act as condensation nuclei for droplets of alcohol vapor to form around. The resulting vapor trail traces the path of otherwise invisible charged particles that can be photographed and studied.

Early cloud chambers relied on the natural cosmic radiation constantly falling on earth to go passing through their experiment. The cloud chamber was used to confirm the existence of antimatter in 1932 with the unexpected tracks of an electron that seemed to curl in the opposite direction. This would turn out to be the first detection of a positron, an anti-electron whose positive electric charge bends its path in the opposite direction as it interacts with matter in the cloud chamber. Cloud chambers were also used to discover the neutron (1932) and the muon (1936).

There are four types of charged particles that can be detected in a cloud chamber, all of which leave distinct tracks based on their properties.

- Alpha particles (α), which are helium nuclei emitted by radioactive atoms and consist of two protons and two neutrons. Because they are bulky and low energy, α particles leave short thick tracks.

- Beta particles (β), which are high-energy electrons or positrons emitted in the decay of radioactive atoms. The light and energetic β particles leave curly paths as they bounce around far more massive atoms and molecules in the chamber.

- Muons, the far more massive cousin of the electron, which can plow through the alcohol vapor leaving distinct long and straight lines.

- Protons from natural cosmic radiation, which are rarer but leave thick ionizing tracks like those left by α particles.

Applying a magnetic field to a cloud chamber also reveals important information about particle properties by causing the path of charged particles to bend or curl perpendicularly to the field. The radii of the curls are proportional to the momentum of a particle, its mass and speed. Therefore, quickly moving and heavy particles create straight and short tracks as they fight the magnetic field, whereas even fast and light particles like electrons are curled to a much greater degree. Relatively slowly moving and light particles, like the electron-positron pair shown in diagram 4.2, produce extremely curled tracks against the magnetic field that bend in opposite directions from one another. We will

look closer at magnetic effects on matter and antimatter
particles next when we explore bubble chambers.

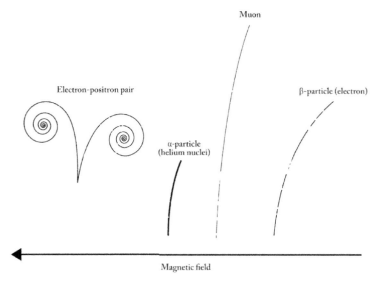

4.2 Cloud chamber tracks left by an electron-positron pair, α-particle, muon
and β-particle (left to right). The paths of particles bend proportionally to their
properties against an applied magnetic field.

Cloud chambers allow a large variety of particles and
processes to be observed in a visual manner and are also
compact and inexpensive to operate. The cloud chamber
was the primary form of particle detector until the 1950s
but lacks the sensitivity of more modern detector designs
and particle tracks can be easily obscured by other incoming
radiation.

Bubble chamber

Like the cloud chamber, bubble chambers also rely on the ability of charged particles to ionize matter, however, the two detectors have distinct differences. Where cloud chambers rely on cooled alcohol vapors, bubble chambers utilize liquids heated to just under their boiling point to produce observable particle tracks. The bubble chamber, first conceived in 1952, was used heavily throughout the 1960s and 70s to discover the charm quark, bottom quark and tau-lepton, the heaviest third-generation cousin of the electron.

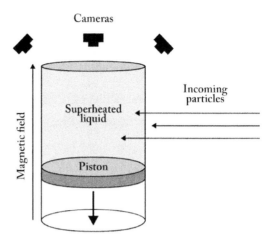

4.3 Bubble chambers use a piston to expand superheated liquids that have been brought to just below boiling point, allowing bubbles to nucleate around the paths of charged particles passing through the liquid.

Bubble chambers consist of a sealed chamber filled with a superheated liquid like hydrogen. A piston allows the liquid in the chamber to be expanded, leaving it in a near-boiling state. A beam of particles, such as protons, is then sent through the expanded liquid which ionizes atoms in the hot liquid, allowing a trail for bubbles to nucleate and condense around, like vapor trails in a cloud chamber. Cameras mounted strategically around the chamber can capture three-dimensional images of particle tracks and interactions that can be used to study their properties and behaviors.

Ultimately, the piston can be used to recompress and reset the heated liquid for detecting the next round of particles. Detection: * The density of bubbles along a track is proportional to the energy lost by the incoming charged particle. Faster and more energetic particles produce dense tracks of bubbles, while those of slower and less energetic particles are sparser.

As with a cloud chamber, a magnetic field can be applied throughout the heated liquid in a bubble chamber which causes the paths of charged particles to bend or curl. This is because the direction of the forces acting on the particle as it moves through the magnetic field are perpendicular to the direction of the field itself and the velocity of the particle. The paths of positively charged particles such as a proton bend to the right against the magnetic field, while negatively charged particles like an electron bend to the left. This can also be useful for identifying antimatter particles, whose opposite charge causes them to bend in the opposite direction of their matter counterpart.

The curve of a track is proportional to the particle's momentum in that less massive particles like electrons are easily affected by magnetic forces, causing their paths to be notably curly. The paths of heavier generations of charged leptons like the muon and tau also curl but to a far lesser degree due to their relatively large masses and therefore greater momenta.

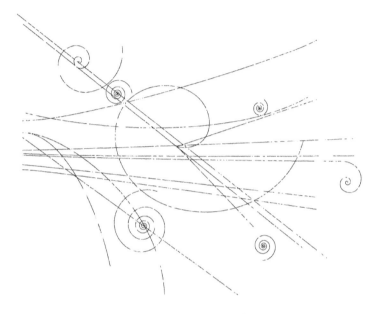

4.4 Example depicting the bending of incoming particles' momentum under the influence of magnetic forces in bubble chamber.

Despite having zero charge neutral particles like photons and neutrons can also be detected in a bubble chamber. While they leave no visible tracks themselves, neutral particles can still interact directly with matter resulting in the production of particle charged pairs that can be observed. Photons, for example, can interact with atoms in the liquid to produce electron-positron pairs which curl in opposite directions forming a V-shape in the detector. Bubble chambers can even be used to indirectly study neutrinos through the particles they produce while interacting with matter in the heated liquid and they were even critical in making important early discoveries about neutrinos, such as the fact that they exist multiple generations or flavors.

While bubble chambers were key to many important discoveries, they also prove relatively expensive, provide comparatively small sample sizes of particles and are slow and inefficient to operate compared to modern detector designs. Both cloud and bubble chambers have long since been replaced by more sophisticated and complex modern detectors that operate on semiconducting materials, primarily silicon.

A simplified example involves two electrodes placed on opposite sides of a microscopic silicon wafer that has been given impurities which cause it to produce an electric field. Charged particles pass through the wafer causing electrons in the silicon atoms to be excited into a higher energy orbital, thereby leaving the absence or "hole" of an electron in the lower energy orbital. The electrons and so-called holes are then attracted to the opposing electrodes, providing a signal that can then be measured. The more energetic the particle, the more electron-hole pairs and therefore the greater signal it will produce in the detector.

The cloud and bubble chambers were both key inventions that allowed for the discovery and study of several new particles. The creators of both devices, C.T.R. Wilson and Donald Glaser were each awarded the 1927 and 1960 Nobel Prizes in Physics for their inventions and resulting contributions. Through the decades, detectors have grown increasingly complex and sophisticated, and can detect far wider ranges of particles which can be studied at far greater resolutions.

Modern particle detectors consist of several layers and types of detectors, each designed to acutely record specific properties and allow them to detect a comparatively huge range of particles. While they vary depending on the type of particle being studied, some of the detectors utilized in modern experiments might include:

Calorimeters: designed to measure a particle's energy by absorbing the particle and measuring the released energy.

Trackers: to determine a particle's path using the ionization process as it passes through the detector. Tracking detectors operate on the same basic principles as cloud and bubble chambers.

Identifiers: for determining the type of particle by measuring its defining properties, such as mass and electric charge.

Cherenkov and scintillators: which operate in a similar manner to neutrino detectors (see previous section).

Depending on the nature of the experiment, many other specialized detectors might also be used to measure momentum, trajectory time, velocity and other important properties. Most importantly, versus operating as standalone equipment to detect naturally occurring cosmic radiation, the variety of modern designs are most often used to detect the particles created in high-energy particle accelerators.

Neutrino detectors

Since neutrinos only interact weakly with other matter, they require their own specialized detectors, which are often constructed deep underground to shield them from cosmic rays and other background radiation that can easily mask weak neutrino interactions. There are two primary types of neutrino detectors, which operate on simple principles:

Water Cherenkov detectors:
Cherenkov radiation occurs when a charged particle travels faster than the speed of light through a medium, like water, causing a disturbance in the electromagnetic field that appears as a visible blue glow. Rare interactions between neutrinos and water produce energetic leptons like electrons or muons that move faster than light through the water, creating Cherenkov radiation. By using large tanks of water lined with sensitive photomultiplier tubes, Cherenkov detectors can convert the resulting Cherenkov radiation into electrical signals that can then be used to retrace the path of the produced charged leptons and determine the flavor of interacting neutrino.

An example of a water Cherenkov detector is *Super-Kamiokande* (or simply *Super-K*), located in a mine a thousand meters below the surface of Japan. Super-K consists of a 40-meter-tall tank holding over 50,000 tons of ultra-pure water and lined with state-of-the-art photomultiplier tubes. As incoming neutrinos from the sun and other powerful astronomical events interact with atoms in the water, they produce high-speed charged particles that create Cherenkov radiation which can then be used to determine neutrino flavor. At 1,000 meters (about 3280.84 ft) below the surface and covered by a thick layer of rock, Super-K is in an ideal location that is sheltered from high-energy cosmic rays and other background radiation that would otherwise easily obscure weak neutrino interactions.

Scintillator detectors:

Similar but less popular, scintillator detectors rely on large tanks of a liquid scintillation medium, which is a material that emits light when ionized by a charged particle. In rare interactions between neutrinos and atoms in the scintillation material, charged particles are produced which then ionize the material, producing scintillation light. As with Cherenkov detectors, photomultiplier tubes around the tank can then convert the scintillation radiation into measurable electrical signals. The recorded signals can be used to determine the properties of the produced charged particles, which can be used to indirectly determine the properties of the interacting neutrino.

Accelerators

As opposed to the elaborate inventions conceived to detect natural and produced particles, the primary goal of particle accelerators is to propel charged particles to near-light speeds to either collide with a target or head-on with other particles. Accelerators can be linear or circular in their design.

Linear accelerators consist of a straight line of cavities that have oscillating electric fields. As charged particles pass through the electric field, they are given energy and are propelled. The frequency of the oscillating electric fields must be carefully synchronized to be in-phase with passing particles, so they are properly propelled as their energy and speed increases with each new cavity. This design means the more energy you wish to give particles, the longer the accelerator must be.

Circular accelerators steer and guide charged particles through electromagnetic fields. Radiation propels the particles and magnetic fields curve their path to send them in a circular path. Unlike linear accelerators that propel particles along a finite line of acceleration cavities, the electromagnetic fields of circular accelerators are carefully designed to continually propel, curve and energize particles with each new loop.

Cyclotrons & synchrotrons

The earliest model of particle accelerator was the *cyclotron*, invented in the 1920s. Cyclotrons contain two D-shaped electrodes called "dees," which are placed in a vacuum chamber and surrounded by a large magnet. Both dees are then connected to an alternating voltage. As particles are injected into the center of the cyclotron, they are accelerated by the alternating voltage between the dees, but their trajectories are curved by the surrounding magnetic field, allowing the particles to travel in a circular path. The frequency of the voltage and cyclotron can be carefully

synchronized so the particles are accelerated and gain
energy each time they pass around the dees. The more
particles are accelerated the harder their energy fights the
magnetic field, gradually increasing their radius. Once
particles have been accelerated and gained enough energy
for their path to reach the outer edges of the dees they are
extracted from the cyclotron for various uses and
applications.

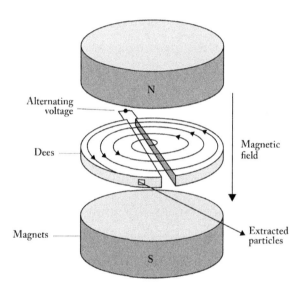

4.5 Basic diagram of simple cyclotron model.

The energetic particles produced in cyclotrons can then be
used to bombard atoms of various elements. The
accelerated particles smash into the atoms with enough

energy to create entirely new but unstable and radioactive isotopes, like Carbon-11, which has six protons and five neutrons and was first produced using a cyclotron in 1934. These radioisotopes, in turn, have a wide variety of important medical applications, such as cancer and brain diagnoses. Many modern hospitals have cyclotrons on premises specifically to produce radioisotopes for many forms of diagnosis and treatment.

The energies achieved by the cyclotron, ranging anywhere from a few to a few hundred MeV, is naturally limited by its design in that particles are eventually forced to be extracted when reaching the edge of the dees. The cyclotron design was later improved into the synchrotron which uses a rapidly oscillating radiofrequency (RF) electric field that can be adjusted to allow particles to remain in a constant circular path. As a result, particles can make continual loops around a synchrotron until they have achieved the desired energy to be extracted. Like cyclotrons, synchrotrons still have several modern medical applications such as medical imaging and cancer treatments. However, while cyclotrons can be small enough to be operated in a room only a few meters wide, synchrotrons are often housed in separate facilities and have diameters of hundreds of meters.

Large Hadron Collider

Though these same basic synchrotron principles still underlie the most powerful modern particle accelerators in the world, the size of the equipment has grown. Most notably, the Large Hadron Collider (LHC), which is a 27 km (17 mi) underground circular detector running below the border of Switzerland and France. As its name insinuates, the LHC collides hadrons, the class of particles composed of quarks, most often protons. Protons acquire 6.5 tera-electronvolts (one trillion electron-volts) of energy as they race around the LHC, which at everyday scales is roughly the same as a safety pin dropped from a couple centimeters. However, when concentrated into the small regions of subatomic particles the energy produced in proton collisions at the LHC is enough to briefly simulate the high-energy conditions in the universe fractions of a second after the Big Bang. The power of the LHC allows for millions of these mini–Big-Bangs to occur every second, each one capable of producing dozens, even hundreds of particles in the process that can be studied to deepen our understanding of the universe at the most fundamental levels.

The relatively gigantic energies achieved by the LHC has allowed the discover or confirmation of countless elementary particles, including the top quark in 1995, the heaviest known elementary particle at more than 170 times the mass of the protons that collide to produce them. The LHC was also responsible for the discovery of the third-generation tau neutrino in 2000, along with several new mesons and baryons. The most widely covered triumph of the Large Hadron Collider occurred in 2012 with the dramatic confirmation of the Higgs boson, which we will discuss in later chapters.

In principle, protons could simply continually accelerate around the LHC, gaining more energy in the process. We find, however, this is far more challenging in practice because of the laws of Albert Einstein's special theory of relativity. In particular, the mass-energy equivalence and resulting equation $E = mc2$, which shows that by being one and the same, mass and energy can be converted into one another, like exchanging two forms of currency with the speed of light squared as the exchange rate. However, because the speed of light is such a large number regardless of which units of measurement are chosen, a relatively gigantic amount of energy is required to propel protons to increasingly greater speeds. The closer protons come to approaching the speed of light, the energy required only becomes compounded based on the laws of special relativity.

While cavities of radiation propel protons around the LCH, powerful superconducting magnets work to bend their paths and steer them in a circular path. The more energy the protons acquire, the more powerful the magnets must become to hold the particles in their paths. Not only does operating the magnets require great amounts of energy, to maintain their superconducting properties they must be kept at around -264° C (-443 ° F), which also requires great energy.

Like any scientific equipment, the LHC and other accelerators can be upgraded and updated to achieve greater energy and allow particles of greater mass to be produced in the process. The LHC itself has received four substantial upgrades since its first run in 2008 that achieved energies of just over 1 TeV. As of 2018, it has been upgraded to now achieve over 13.5 TeV.

Exotic particles

Beyond the building blocks of ordinary matter

Strangeness

During the 1940s and 50s when particle physics was still in its infancy, physicists had been using cloud chambers to carefully study the natural cosmic radiation constantly bombarding our planet and interacting with particles in the atmosphere. This would lead to the discovery of a bizarre new particle called the k-meson, or simply *kaon* (*K*), which created V-shaped tracks in the detector as they decayed. The oddity was that despite their large mass, which was measured at nearly 500 MeV, and therefore being highly unstable, kaons seemed to have a lifetime of around a hundred times longer than predicted. Other particles soon emerged that exhibited the same behavior, which was appropriately named *strangeness*.

Today we know that strangeness arises from the internal quark makeup of all hadrons containing at least one strange or anti-strange quark, the lightest of the two heavier quark generations. This also means there exist both strange mesons and strange baryons. The kaon mentioned previously, for instance, contains one strange quark and one normal quark, either up or down. This also allows for four possible states based on electric charge, shown in table 4.1. With their opposite net charges, the K^+ and K^- serve as each other's antiparticles. The two possible K^0 states are both electrically neutral but are distinguishable through their decay paths.

Kaon	Quark content	Charge	Mass	Decay path
K⁺	US	+1	1,115.7 MeV	p + π– or n + π
K⁻	US	-1	1,189.4 MeV	p + π0
K⁰	DS	0	1,197.4 MeV	n + π–
K⁰	DS	0	1,192.6 MeV	n + π0

TABLE 4.1 Possible states and associated decay paths of the kaon.

What makes "strange" particles so unusual is that while they are produced through strong interactions like high-energy collisions in cosmic rays and particle accelerators, they are only able to decay weakly. This is what leads to the abnormally long lifetime of strange particles since undergoing a weak interaction is simply such an unlikely event by comparison.

Just like energy, electric charge, strangeness is quantized and can be assigned integer values of -1, 0 or +1. The total strangeness of any particle, like a kaon, is determined by the sum of the strangeness values of its individual quarks. The stable first-generation up and down quarks, as well as the heavier and unstable charm, bottom and top quarks all have a strangeness of 0, as do each of their associated antiparticles. The strange quark itself, alternatively, has a strangeness of -1 and the anti-strange quark has a strangeness of +1. The +1 strangeness of the K+, for instance, can be found by adding the 0 strangeness of its constituent up quark and the +1 strangeness of its anti-strange quark.

There are many possible combinations of strange mesons beyond the kaon, some examples of which are listed in table 4.2.

Strange meson	Symbol	Quark content	Mass	Decay path
D meson	D	CD/CU	1,869.4 MeV	K + π
Eta	η	UU/DD/S S	547.9 MeV	π + π
Phi	φ	SS	1019.4 MeV	K + K

TABLE 4.2 Common examples of strange mesons along with their quark content and associated decay modes.

In addition to strange mesons there are also strange baryons, which are known as *hyperons* and contain at least one strange quark but no heavier charm, top or bottom quarks, simply because they are too massive and would decay far too quickly.

As with kaons, the internal quark composition of a hyperon also determines its possible decay paths and can also allow for electrically charged and neutral versions. Specifically, there are four types of hyperons, known as the lambda (Λ), sigma (Σ), xi (Ξ) and omega (Ω), shown in table 4.3, along with their quark content and associated decay paths:

Hyperon	Symbol	Quark content	Mass	Decay path

Lambda	Λ	UDS	1,115.7 MeV	p + π– or n + π
Sigma	Σ+	UUS	1,189.4 MeV	p + π0
Sigma	Σ-	DDS	1,197.4 MeV	n + π–
Sigma	Σ0	UDS	1,192.6 MeV	n + π0
Xi	Ξ-	DSS	1,321.7 MeV	$\Lambda^0 + \pi^-$
Xi	Ξ0	USS	1,314.9 MeV	$\Lambda^0 + \pi^0$
Omega	Ω-	SSS	1,672.5 MeV	$\Lambda^0 + \pi^-$

TABLE 4.3 Possible hyperon states along with their associated quark content and decay modes.

In all case, hyperons always decay into to a stable baryon, either a proton, neutron or lambda in the case of the Ξ and Ω, along with one or more additional particles. Throughout the 1950s, physicists would observe the same outcome in all strong and electromagnetic interactions, the number of baryons always seemed to be preserved. This would ultimately lead to the introduction of an important new quantum number, called baryon number. Like electric charge, a particle's baryon number can be one of three possible quantized values, +1, -1 and 0. Baryons themselves have a baryon number of +1, antibaryons -1, and all other particles are designated as 0. In this way, the total number of baryons and antibaryons must always remain the same before and after all interactions in nature, even weak interactions.

Take a beta-minus decay, for example, in which a neutron decays into a proton, and electron and an antineutrino. Both the neutron and the proton it decays into have a baryon number of +1, and since the electron and antineutrino both have a baryon number of 0, the total baryon number before and after the interaction is conserved.

Like all conserved properties, baryon number is valuable for determining the outcomes of various fundamental particle interactions. However, it also helps to tell us about the nature of matter and the infant universe. While equal amounts of matter and antimatter are believed to have been created in the Big Bang, the universe we observe today is composed overwhelmingly of matter and a comparatively minuscule amount of antimatter. While the exact reasons for this asymmetry are currently unclear, the conservation of baryon number has ensured that this disparity in favor of matter has remained constant over billions of years. Were baryon number not conserved, all matter and antimatter would have annihilated, making the universe as we know it impossible in the first place.

Resonances

Just like electrons can absorb and gain energy, moving them to a higher orbital and leaving the atom in an excited state, baryons like protons and neutrons also exist in excited states known as a resonance. Resonances are often produced in the high-energy collisions of particle accelerators but can also be created when the constituent quarks of a nucleon absorb enough energy to be in an excited state. As with the excited states of atoms, resonances are very unstable and have remarkably short lifetimes before decaying back into their ground state nucleon and various mesons. Versus the many weak decays we have encountered, resonances often decay via the strong interaction.

A common example of such a resonance is the delta (Δ), an excited baryon that can exist in three states based on electric charge, Δ^+, Δ^- or Δ^0. The excited delta baryon is very unstable and exists for only 5.6×10^{-24} seconds before typically decaying back into a nucleon and a pion. However, delta resonances also have less common decay modes in which they decay into a nucleon and kaon. In all cases, baryon number remains conserved.

The omega hyperon briefly discussed in the previous section is also an example of a baryon in an excited state. Composed of three strange quarks that share a powerful strong mutual bond, the omega is the most stable of the hyperons with a lifetime of roughly 10^{-10} seconds before decaying into a Λ^0 and π^-.

Resonances are not limited to only baryons and can also occur in mesons, which are excited states of the constituent quark-antiquark pairs. As with baryons, meson resonances are unstable and quickly decay back to their ground states. A few common examples of the many possible meson resonances are shown in table 4.4.

Resonance	Symbol	Quark content	Mass	Decay path
Rho	ρ	UDS	1,115.7 MeV	$p + \pi-$ or n $+ \pi$
Omega	ω	SSS	1,672.5 MeV	$\Lambda^0 + \pi^-$
Phi	φ	SS	1,019.4 MeV	$K^+ + K^-$

TABLE 4.4 Common examples of baryon and meson resonances.

The Standard Model of Particle Physics

Our unified framework of matter and forces

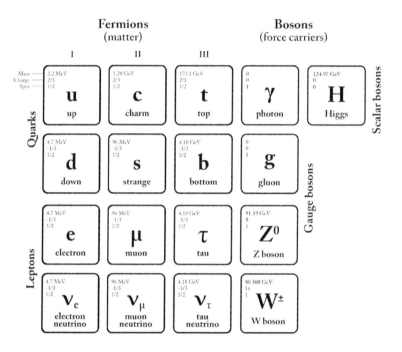

All the way from the elementary building blocks of matter and their properties and behaviors to the fundamental interactions in nature, we have been gradually working toward a general understanding of the ***standard model of particle physics***, or simply the "standard model." The standard model is our grand masterpiece description of the elementary particles of nature and the fundamental interactions they undergo; it is a collection of the many scientific and mathematical frameworks that have developed rapidly since the start of the twentieth century, all underpinned and governed by the laws of both quantum mechanics and the special theory of relativity.

The standard model categorizes all particles in nature into two broad categories, fermions and bosons, which have been the two primary focuses of our discussions thus far. Fermions are the elementary building blocks of matter and include all generations of leptons, quarks and neutrinos. All fermions, as we learned in chapter two, have half integer spins and are therefore subject to the exclusion principle, prohibiting any two of them to exist simultaneously in an identical quantum state and allowing for the structure of matter. Bosons are the force-carrying particles that mediate the fundamental interactions of nature, including the photon that mediates all electromagnetic interactions, the gluons that strongly bind quarks into hadrons and mesons and the W and Z bosons mediating all weak interactions.

Above all else, any scientific theory or framework is only as strong as its predictions and is therefore under the constant scrutiny of evermore precise experimental methods. The standard model describes nature at the fundamental level to exquisite degrees of accuracy that has been repeatedly upheld by all experimental data. It can, for example, predict the magnetic strength of the electron to an accuracy of 14 decimal places against what we measure experimentally.

However, the success of the standard model does not simply describe particles and interactions but has been responsible for predicting its share of particles prior to being discovered experimentally. The W and Z bosons that mediate weak interactions, the second-generation strange and charm quarks, the third-generation top quark and the third-generation tau neutrino were all predicted by the standard model. The experimental confirmation of these particles, which we will discuss while exploring detectors and accelerators, helped to cement and verify the predictive power of the standard model.

Symmetry

Successfully as the Standard Model has held up against experimental rigor, like all scientific theories, the entire framework relies critically on certain assumptions about how nature works and should even one of these assumptions prove to be untrue, the entire framework becomes a broken unworthy description of the universe.

Specifically, the Standard Model as an entire framework is based on the idea that nature operates in a symmetrical way. In the most general sense, symmetry occurs when something remains unchanged or invariant under various transformations. Symmetry manifests itself in a variety of ways and places in nature, depending on the type of transformation.

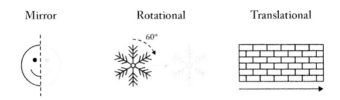

6.1 Common examples of mirror, rotational and translational symmetry in nature.

Mirror symmetry: when an object can be divided into two equal halves. Leaves, the bodies of bacteria and even the human face can all be considered as roughly mirror symmetric.

Rotational symmetry: remaining invariant under rotation. A sphere is an example of perfect rotational symmetry since it can be turned by all 360 degrees and its appearance remains identical. A snowflake, on the other hand, has a six-fold rotational symmetry in which it will appear identical with each turn of 60 degrees.

Translational symmetry: invariance when being shifted by a certain distance in a certain direction. The pattern of a brick wall, for instance, remains invariant as you move along the direction of the wall. Translational symmetry is also used in many fabric patterns and textiles. This form of invariance applies to translations in both space and time.

Symmetry is not only important to our sense of style and beauty, but also to the laws of nature themselves. Profound mathematical connections exist between conserved quantities in nature, like energy and momentum, and natural symmetries. Specifically, now named after its discoverer, **Noether's theorem** shows us that each conserved quantity correlates directly to a specific symmetry. Some examples of this are as follows:

Time translation symmetry: if the laws of physics are invariant at all points in time, energy is conserved.

Spatial translation symmetry: if the laws of physics are invariant at all positions in space, linear momentum is conserved.

Rotational symmetry: if the laws of physics are invariant under rotation, angular momentum is conserved.

Gauge invariance

Just like properties, conservation laws and several other factors, symmetries help us understand the laws of nature and provide important predictive power for our theories. As opposed to the common ideas of symmetry with which we are most familiar, the symmetries in nature become considerably more abstract and subtle at the subatomic level.

The standard model is based on the principles of gauge invariance or simply gauge symmetry. The term "gauge" refers to the freedom, or rather the choice by which a theory allows a physical system, like particles and their interactions, to be described. Gauge symmetry ensures that regardless of which way a system is explained, the end results remain the same, or invariant. Gauge symmetry is also a significant underlying component of the standard model. Just as classical physics allows us to describe the processes of the macroscopic world from all reference frames using the same fundamental laws, gauge symmetry allows us to describe the elementary particles of nature and their interactions from all vantage points using the same laws and principles underlying the standard model of particle physics.

Further, the standard model relies on local gauge symmetry, a specific application of gauge symmetry which allows the fundamental fields to vary across space and time without changing the observed results. For instance, the electric and magnetic fields around a charged object like an electron can be represented accurately in a multitude of ways but still describe the same electromagnetic interaction, the way two individuals can witness an automobile crash, and each describe it accurately using two different languages.

CPT symmetry

As the framework of quantum field theory developed other fundamental symmetries soon emerged. Three formerly independent forms of symmetry, charge conjugation, parity and time reversal, gradually revealed themselves to be an important interconnected property of nature.

Charge conjugation (C) is the transformation that reverses the sign of the electric charge for all the particles in a system, effectively changing them into their associated antiparticle. An example would be changing a negative electron into a positron.

Parity (P) is the spatial inversion of a system, which transforms its x, y and z coordinates to their opposite -x, -y and -z, effectively producing the exact "mirror" of the system.

Time reversal (T) observes the symmetry of a system under the opposite direction of time, like watching a movie clip in reverse. Under this transformation, the velocities, spin and interactions of all particles in the system are reversed.

In essence, CPT symmetry states that even when you switch the electric charge, the spatial orientation and direction of time, the laws of physics will remain unchanged. As of this writing, no experimental evidence has been shown to disprove the fundamental symmetry between charge conjugation, parity and time reversal.

Oddly, however, certain particle interactions, mostly involving the weak decay of particles such as neutral kaons, have been observed to violate the symmetry between charge conjugation and parity. In other words, the transformation of particles into their associated antiparticles does not always occur perfectly symmetrically under the mirror image of a system. While such observed CP violations have been incorporated successfully into the standard model, the exact origins are still an active area of research and are important for further understanding the nature of CPT symmetry.

Electroweak unification

Symmetries are also useful for identifying otherwise hidden or obscure relationships between the fundamental interactions in nature, allowing them to be unified or described by a single framework. The most familiar unification was of electricity and magnetism, which had been studied as two distinct phenomena for centuries but were ultimately shown to be the closely related result of interconnected fields, all of which is described by a single electromagnetic theory. As the standard model developed and its predictive powers became increasingly powerful, physicists noticed certain similarities between the electromagnetic and weak forces, which seems peculiar considering one mediates interactions between charged particles and the other mediates the decay of particles. Yet, undeniable similarities were found to exist in the mathematical structure describing the two interactions, hinting at a connection between them.

These similarities allowed physicists to develop a single unified framework for describing both the electromagnetic and weak forces, which relates them through their mathematical symmetries to describe them as two manifestations of an even more fundamental underlying force known as the ***electroweak*** interaction.

During the first fractions of a second after the Big Bang, electroweak theory predicts that the electromagnetic and weak force would have appeared perfectly indistinguishable from one another. As the universe expanded and cooled, the similarities between the two interactions began to dissipate, allowing the electromagnetic and weak forces manifest in their two expected distinct manners.

Most notably, electroweak theory predicts that the virtual bosons mediating each interaction, the photons mediating electromagnetic interactions and the W and Z bosons mediating weak interactions, would have been completely massless during these initial moments of the universe. While all experimental data does seem to indicate that the photon is indeed massless, it shows the exact opposite for the W and Z, both of which have relatively gigantic masses, upward of 80 to 90 times that of a proton. As we discovered, these vastly different masses, in accordance with the uncertainty principle, were what allowed the electromagnetic force to have an infinite range but restricted the weak force to acting only over the ultra-short distances of a single hadron. If electroweak theory is considered correct, which it is, then why did some particles like the photon remain eternally massless, while other particles like the W, Z and many others did not? How do the W and Z bosons, predicted by the standard model to be completely massless, spontaneously gain the masses that we measure experimentally? Or, to pose the more fundamental question: how do any of the elementary particles of the standard model acquire their mass?

Just like an automobile itself is not capable of getting you to your destination and requires fuel to do so, the standard model requires certain inputs before it can make its precision predictions and is not capable of doing so by itself. In fact, it requires more than a dozen inputs to successfully make its predictions, including fundamental constants in nature like the speed of light (c) and Planck's constant (h). Perhaps most notably, the standard model requires experimental data about mass and cannot predict the mass of any elementary particles by itself.

Higgs mechanism

In 1964, Belgian physicists, François Englert and Robert Brout, and independently English physicist, Peter Higgs, all proposed a similar solution in the form of an additional quantum field, now referred to as the Higgs field, permeating all of space and time, in which interactions with the field provide the mechanism by which the fundamental particles of nature acquire their mass.

As with all quantum fields, the standard model also predicts an associated exchange particle that mediates all interactions with the Higgs field, fittingly named the ***Higgs boson***. As a boson, the Higgs has zero spin, meaning it is not subject to the exclusion principle and may exist in an identical quantum state to other Higgs particles. The mass of the Higgs boson, on the other hand, which is roughly 125 GeV, dwarfs even the mass of the W and Z bosons. This also makes the Higgs extremely unstable, only existing for in the range of 10^{-22} before decaying into lighter and more stable particles. The decay modes undergone by the Higgs boson are determined by the particles with which it interacts. Between its tremendous mass and remarkably short lifetime, detecting the Higgs boson proves to be an incredibly challenging task. The laws of special relativity, in particular $E = mc^2$, reveal that comparatively tremendous quantities of energy are required to produce even a particle of modest mass, let alone one well over a hundred GeV. Our most state-of-the-art accelerators were incapable of such energies until well into the twenty-first century.

Even still, in the high-energy conditions produced in accelerator collisions, the creation of a Higgs boson is a relatively rare event. Not to mention, the plethora of other particles produced in such collisions only further obscure potential observations. Couple all of this with the fact that the Higgs decays into other more common particles essentially instantly after being created, detecting one of these bosons is no simple matter, which is why it took until 2012 to officially announce to the world the first experimental confirmation of the Higgs boson.

Spontaneous symmetry breaking

Like all fields, the Higgs field contains a certain amount of potential or stored energy. In the case of the Higgs field, its potential energy curve takes on a unique shape that is often compared to a Mexican sombrero, consisting of a round slope in the center like the crown and a surrounding circular valley like the brim of the hat. The Higgs field is unique from other quantum fields in that it contains non-zero energy even in its ground state. We know that quantum field theory predicts that all fields are teeming with fluctuations of virtual particle-antiparticle pairs popping in an out of existence. However, in the end, these pairs of virtual particles all total to a net-zero energy for the field's ground state. Alternatively, even when absent of any particles or interactions, the Higgs field still possesses considerable amounts of potential energy, around 246 GeV specifically.

To better visualize this scenario, the energy state of the Higgs field can be represented by an imaginary ball residing somewhere on the hat. However, it is very important to note that this does not represent a physical shape in space, but rather the curve of the potential field energy. Nevertheless, treating the scenario physically will help us better understand the mechanisms metaphorically.

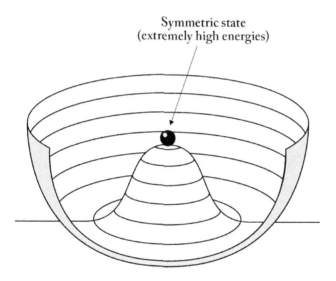

6.2 Under the high-energy conditions of the newborn universe, the potential energy of the Higgs field is predicted to have been in a symmetric state across all of space, or "sitting atop the crown of the hat."

When the ball (the field energy value) sits atop the rounded crown of the hat, the field is at zero and the Higgs field is in a symmetric state. The symmetry of this state lies in the fact that sitting at the smooth spherical tip of the hat, the ball has the potential to roll in any given direction into the brim. In the extremely high-energy earliest moments of the universe, the Higgs field is predicted to have been in such a symmetrical state at every point, preventing it from interacting with particles and thereby allowing them to remain massless. This symmetrical state of the Higgs field under high-energy conditions is also how the bosons mediating both the electromagnetic and weak interactions are massless under the predictions of electroweak theory.

However, as the newborn universe rapidly expanded and cooled, energy scales decreased, eventually reducing to a point in which the Higgs field underwent a phase transition, much like liquid water suddenly begins entering a frozen state at $0°$ C ($32°$ F). As a result, the ball is now forced roll in some direction down into the circular valley of the hat's brim and settles into a ground state with a non-zero energy. As a result of "selecting" a particular direction of the field's energy potential, the original pristine symmetry of the ball sitting atop the hat poised to head in all directions equally is spontaneously broken.

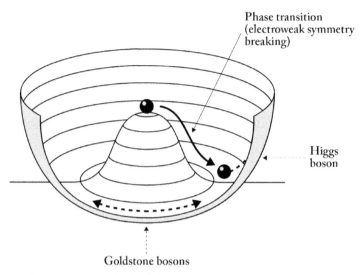

6.3 Decreasing energy levels of the expanding universe caused the symmetry to spontaneously break, causing the field's potential energy value to "roll down" into the "brim of the hat."

Now residing in the circular valley of the hat's brim, new degrees of freedom are introduced to the energy state of the field, four to be exact. Three of the new degrees of freedom manifest themselves as new particles, which on account of Noether's theorem must be massless and are known as *Goldstone bosons*. Importantly, Goldstone bosons do not exist as real observable particles, but rather brief quantum fluctuations, like the remnants of the symmetry breaking process. The massless Goldstone bosons are rapidly absorbed by other particles, namely W and Z bosons.

However, the bosons do not get "absorbed" in the typical sense of disappearing, but rather undergo a complex and abstract process of combining with the states of the W and Z particles. This process of combining with Goldstone bosons provides additional polarizations which allow the otherwise massless W and Z particles to interact with the non-zero energy of the Higgs field and acquire their mass. This overall Higgs mechanism provides the spontaneous breaking of the electroweak symmetry.

The final degree of freedoms manifests as the infamous Higgs boson, which itself interacts heavily with the Higgs field to acquire its relatively large 125 GeV mass. The Higgs boson can also absorb and exchange Goldstone bosons, which further contributes to the acquired masses of the W and Z during spontaneous symmetry breaking. All other massive elementary particles, such as electrons and quarks, now constantly interact directly with the asymmetric and non-zero energy of the Higgs field through the exchange of Higgs bosons. Even as forces are applied to elementary particles, their otherwise light speed velocity is effectively stifled and slowed by their constant interactions with the non-zero energy of the Higgs field, producing the effects of inertial mass (resistance to change in motion). The 2012 experimental confirmation of the Higgs boson at the CERN marked the scientific proof for the existence of the Higgs field, the dramatic vindication of the Higgs mechanism for the origins of mass and rounded out the standard model of particle physics.

Beyond the standard model

Frontiers in modern particle physics

Despite the utter success of the standard model to make highly accurate predictions about nature, it is a notoriously incomplete model. One reason is that the very properties of the building blocks of matter, like energies, electric charge, magnetic effects and more, are under the constant scrutiny of ever finer experimental rigor, and their quantitative values are therefore being continually updated. Considering this, the very predictions of the standard model itself, which rely critically on input pertaining to these quantities, are also in a natural state of constant evolution over time.

Most importantly, a complete description of nature must account for both matter and all the four fundamental forces. The standard model omits and provides no theoretical framework for significant factors of both the building blocks of matter as well as the fundamental forces, namely gravity. While it stands proudly as our most successful description of nature at fundamental scales, it is worth briefly exploring some of the most glaring missing pieces that remain unaccounted for

Dark matter

The standard model provides a remarkably accurate fundamental description of the baryonic matter throughout the universe, comprised of protons, neutrons and electrons, from you and I to planets and stars. Yet, when taking the entirety of this matter into account on cosmological scales, we find that such "ordinary" or familiar matter that we observe only accounts for a shockingly small portion of the total matter we measure throughout the universe, roughly 15% specifically. This indicates that well over 80% of the universe is composed of some form of invisible and yet undetectable matter that does not undergo any electromagnetic interaction, including with light. This predominant yet unidentified form of matter goes by the collective name *dark matter*.

Dark matter reveals its presence on astronomical scales, as with the motions of stars and galaxies, for instance. The carefully observed rotational speeds of the stars in distant galaxies cannot be accounted for based on the gravitational effects from ordinary matter alone, indicating the presence of some additional yet unobserved mass. Even the motions of entire clusters of galaxies remain unexplained by the observed matter in the universe and can only be accounted for by incorporating dark matter. Several models and theories have been put forth to account for dark matter currently, most of which take us beyond the scope of our discussions. Nevertheless, it is worth gaining a general understanding for some of the primary candidates, some of which include:

WIMPs (*Weakly Interacting Massive Particles*): As their name insinuates, WIMPs are hypothetical elementary particles that possess mass, but only interact very weakly with ordinary baryonic matter. In fact, they are predicted to have a mass several times that of a proton, hence their significant gravitational contributions in observations. Simply by virtue of the "weak" interactions relatively low coupling strength compared to the other forces, detecting WIMPs experimentally proves extremely challenging. Detecting their presence indirectly through small anomalies in the motion of stars, or far below ground as they pass through Earth are ongoing, and so far, unsuccessful searches. Like other particles of the standard model, WIMPs are believed to have been created during the earliest high-energy moments after the Big Bang.

Axions: First proposed in the 1970s to explain potential violations of symmetries in certain strong nuclear interactions among quarks, axions are predicted to be extremely lightweight particles that interact only very weakly with other matter. Predicted ranges for the potential mass of the axion, by some measures, also align well with predicted mass ranges for dark matter. Further, some theoretical models predict that tremendous quantities of axions would have been produced in the early inflationary moments after the Big Bang, supporting the abundance of dark matter we observe cosmologically today. Each of these factors has made the axion an enticing candidate for dark matter in more recent decades.

Sterile neutrinos: We have already encountered the three "flavors" of neutrinos associated with each generation of lepton in the standard model; the electron neutrino, muon neutrino and tau neutrino. In addition to the three standard model neutrinos, so-called "sterile" neutrinos are a hypothetical additional class of neutrino that do not even interact weakly, but only gravitationally, making them extraordinarily challenging to detect by current standards. Some models allow for the existence of a sterile version of all three neutrino flavors, I.e., a sterile electron, muon and tau neutrino.

The existence of dark matter was first predicted in the early 1930s, and the search for its identity has continued steadily since. From dedicated detectors, shielded from cosmic rays deep under the Earth's surface, to experimental data from high-energy particle collisions, no form of dark matter detection has proven successful. As of this writing, no conclusive experimental evidence — direct or indirect — has been collected, making dark matter and most of the matter in the universe at large a complete mystery.

Dark energy

We have also explored energy at the fundamental level throughout our discussions. All the matter and energy in the universe has been in a state of rapid expansion since the moment of the Big Bang. The mass of this expanding matter also produces attractive gravitational forces. The more the universe expands, the farther diluted and diffuse the matter and energy become and the more the far-reaching forces of gravity should take control. As a result, the expansion of the universe itself should, over cosmological time scales, begin to slow and ultimately contract as the expansive forces of matter and energy succumb to the pull of gravity. Moreover, cosmological models indicate that this was, in fact, the case and the expansion of the universe was slowing down until roughly 5 billion years ago when the expansion began to accelerate. This was first revealed through observations of distant supernovae (the violent end-of-life explosions of distant stars) at the end of the twentieth century.

Yet, as was the case with ordinary matter, the net amount of energy we measure throughout the known universe can only account for around 30% of the energy required to explain the observed rate of expansion. This indicates the presence of some form of unidentified or dark energy causing the universe to expand at an ever-increasing rate, and in turn, means nearly 70% of the universe's net energy goes unaccounted for by the standard model, as it currently stands.

The properties and nature of dark energy are poorly understood at the present and are the subject of ongoing debate and research. From its observed effects on the universe, we know it must exert a negative pressure, allowing it to act directly against the gravitational forces of matter. One of the leading explanations for dark energy has been found in the resurrection of a formerly abandoned idea from the early twentieth century. While formulating his flagship general theory of relativity to describe the universal laws of gravity, Albert Einstein introduced to his equations a mathematical term known as the ***cosmological constant***, denoted by the Greek symbol lambda, Λ. In essence, Λ allows for a constant energy density that remains homogeneous throughout space even as the universe expands. While Einstein introduced this term to allow for a static universe, it was then quickly withdrawn upon the discovery that our universe is expanding as of the 1920s. In fact, Einstein notoriously and playfully referred to the addition of Λ to his equations as his "greatest blunder."

In recent years, Einstein's cosmological constant has received renewed interest as a candidate for — or at least factor in — dark energy. In this sense, a constant and homogeneous energy is simply an innate property of the universe, working to automatically force space apart, effectively acting as a natural anti-gravity.

Another model considers dark energy as a dynamic field, called the quintessence, permeating all of space, that unlike the cosmological constant, can vary from one region to another. Over cosmological time scales, the evolution of the field can ultimately lead to the changing strength of dark matter, supporting the observed fact that universal expansion is accelerating over time.

Still, other models demand that we rethink our entire idea and concept of gravity, which would require substantial updates or the complete disregard of general relativity, which by all measures has proven to be accurate to an astonishingly high degree. As of this writing, the search to identify and describe dark energy is ongoing and is currently not accounted for in any way by the standard model.

Quantum gravity

The most glaring missing piece of the standard model of particle physics is gravity, the fourth and most directly familiar of the fundamental forces of nature. Under no circumstances is the force of gravity mentioned or taken into consideration by the standard model in its current state, even indirectly. There are many well-known reasons for this omission, most notably that general relativity describes gravitational effects on vast cosmological scales, whereas quantum mechanics describes the ultra-small.

There are also striking differences in how we describe gravity versus the other three fundamental forces of nature.

By 1915, Einstein expanded the laws of his successful special theory of relativity to account for the effects of gravity and acceleration, which he showed to be manifestations of the same underlying phenomenon. General relativity still stands as our grand framework for describing the universal laws of gravity, in the same way the standard model is the framework for describing the electroweak and strong forces. However, general relativity describes all gravitational effects as the result of curvatures in the fabric of space itself, or more appropriately the unified *spacetime*. Specifically, the presence of mass and energy causes indentations in spacetime, often analogously compared to the indentations created in a thin stretched rubber sheet by a heavy ball. Such a mechanism, in and of itself, differs significantly from the way we describe the other three fundamental forces of nature.

7.1 Albert Einstein's general theory of relativity describes gravitational forces as arising from the presence of mass and energy creating curvatures in spacetime itself.

The intricate mathematics of general relativity characterize these curvatures or bends in spacetime as smooth continuous, with changes occurring seamlessly from one point to the next, rather like descriptions of energy in classical mechanics. However, we know undoubtedly from the laws of quantum mechanics that nature occurs in discrete quantized states at fundamental scales, including the force fields themselves. The very continuous versus discrete nature of the two frameworks are in direct contradiction of one another.

Further, the development of quantum field theory describes all fundamental interactions in nature through the rapid exchange of virtual bosons that are excited states of the underlying field. Conceptually, describing forces as curvatures in spacetime and particle exchanges are entirely different methodologies. Though quantum mechanical models have been proposed that predict a massless boson called the graviton as the particle mediating gravitational interaction, no direct or indirect evidence for such a particle has been found to date.

As mentioned earlier in our discussions, the relative coupling strength of gravity is 10^{-33} times weaker than the electromagnetic force. Studying the effects of gravity among the tiny scales atom and subatomic particles is currently not possible experimentally. Reconciling general relativity with the laws of quantum mechanics, thereby unifying all four fundamental forces of nature, is arguably the most important challenge to modern physics and serves as the overarching goal of most theory and research. Among the myriad current theories for quantum gravity, string theory and loop quantum gravity are among the most widely supported, though, neither framework has collected any substantial experimental evidence as of this writing. Both string theory and loop quantum gravity are beyond the scope of our discussions, and each require dedicated focus, but are highly recommended as areas of study.

Index

Printed in Great Britain
by Amazon

39326643R00098